Basketball

DIANE YANCEY

LUCENT BOOKS
A part of Gale, Cengage Learning

GALE
CENGAGE Learning™

Detroit • New York • San Francisco • New Haven, Conn • Waterville, Maine • London

LIBRARY OF CONGRESS CATALOGING-IN-PUBLICATION DATA

Yancey, Diane.
  Basketball / by Diane Yancey.
    p. cm. — (The science behind sports)
  Includes bibliographical references and index.
  ISBN 978-1-4205-0293-0 (hardcover)
  1. Basketball—Juvenile literature. 2. Sports sciences—Juvenile literature. I. Title.
  GV885.1.Y36 2011
  796.323—dc22

                                        2010035239

Lucent Books
27500 Drake Rd
Farmington Hills MI 48331

ISBN-13: 978-1-4205-0293-0
ISBN-10: 1-4205-0293-X

Printed in the United States of America
3 4 5 6 7 14 13 12 11

TABLE OF CONTENTS

FOREWORD

On March 21, 1970, Slovenian ski jumper Vinko Bogataj took a terrible fall while competing at the Ski-flying World Championships in Oberstdorf, West Germany. Bogataj's pinwheeling crash was caught on tape by an ABC *Wide World of Sports* film crew and eventually became synonymous with "the agony of defeat" in competitive sporting. While many viewers were transfixed by the severity of Bogataj's accident, most were not aware of the biomechanical and environmental elements behind the skier's fall—heavy snow and wind conditions that made the ramp too fast and Bogataj's inability to maintain his center of gravity and slow himself down. Bogataj's accident illustrates that, no matter how mentally and physically prepared an athlete may be, scientific principles—such as momentum, gravity, friction, and aerodynamics—always have an impact on performance.

Lucent Books' Science Behind Sports series explores these and many more scientific principles behind some of the most popular team and individual sports, including baseball, hockey, gymnastics, wrestling, swimming, and skiing. Each volume in the series focuses on one sport or group of related sports. The volumes open with a brief look at the featured sport's origins, history and changes, then move on to cover the biomechanics and physiology of playing, related health and medical concerns, and the causes and treatment of sports-related injuries.

In addition to learning about the arc behind a curve ball, the impact of centripetal force on a figure skater, or how water buoyancy helps swimmers, Science Behind Sports readers will also learn how exercise, training, warming up, and diet and nutrition directly relate to peak performance and enjoyment of the sport. Volumes may also cover why certain sports are popular, how sports function in the business world, and which hot sporting issues—sports doping and cheating, for example—are in the news.

Basic physical science concepts, such as acceleration, kinetics, torque, and velocity, are explained in an engaging and accessible manner. The full-color text is augmented by fact boxes, sidebars, photos, and detailed diagrams, charts and graphs. In addition, a subject-specific glossary, bibliography and index provide further tools for researching the sports and concepts discussed throughout Science Behind Sports.

CHAPTER 1

Peach Baskets and Playoffs

For basketball fans, March Madness is a highlight of every spring. For three weeks in March, they sit glued to their TVs as the best college basketball teams in the United States go head-to-head in national playoffs. During the final championship game, people throw basketball-themed parties from New York City to San Francisco. Afterward, fans of the winning team take to the streets to celebrate. At times, feelings get so high that riots break out.

Two months later the same frenzy is repeated with the National Basketball Association (NBA) championships. Again, fans go all out, spending time and money to take part in widespread partying. Long-time Boston Celtics fan Nick Abisi traveled almost one thousand miles from his home in Indianapolis to celebrate in Boston when his favorite team won the NBA championship in 2008. "This is not a team; it's a way of life," he said. "I wouldn't miss this for the world. The smile won't come off my face for months."[1]

Physical education teacher James Naismith never dreamed that basketball would be so popular when he tacked two peach baskets to the balcony of a Springfield, Massachusetts, YMCA gym on December 21, 1891. All he was worried about was controlling a rowdy class of young male executive secretaries who were bored with the gymnastics, calisthenics (exercises such as jumping jacks, sit-ups, and push-ups), and children's games that the Y offered during the cold, snowy days of winter. He later recalled, "The invention of basketball was not an accident. It was developed to meet a need. Those boys simply would not play 'Drop the Handkerchief.'"[2]

Made in America

Before 1891 basketball did not exist. And when his superiors asked him to create a new game, Naismith did not immediately think of throwing balls into baskets. But he wanted to come up with something that was interesting, easy to learn, and safe to play indoors. It was also important that the game involve skill rather than mindless scuffling. He said, "It is our place to encourage games that may be played by gentlemen in a manly way, and show them that science is superior to brute force."[3]

Half-bushel peach baskets served as the first basketball hoops.

So he reviewed other games that were popular at the time. These included rugby, hockey, soccer, football, and lacrosse, the latter a sport of Native American origin. All involved two teams moving a ball back and forth on a field or court to get it to a goal. Naismith decided his game would be similar. To eliminate unnecessary pushing and shoving to get the ball into the goals, however, he decided to place them above head height. He also decided to use a relatively soft soccer ball, so that players would not be hurt if it hit them.

At Naismith's request the Y's janitor made a search for suitable boxes that could be used as goals. There were none in the Y's basement, but he found two half-bushel peach baskets. They would do, Naismith decided. An elevated track formed a gallery ten feet above the gymnasium floor, and a basket could be nailed to the railing at each end. With the baskets in place, the game of basketball was born.

An Instant Hit

With baskets and a ball, Naismith sat down to create the rules of the game. The ball should not be bounced, he decided. It could only be passed from player to player. There could be no walking or running with the ball. The player had to throw it from the spot on which he caught it. A point would be scored each time the ball went into the basket and stayed there. Rough play such as pushing, tripping, or holding an opponent would be a foul, and the offender would be sent from the court. An umpire would ensure fair play. The game would be short—just thirty minutes with a five-minute rest break between halves—with no limit on the size of the team. "The more players, the more fun," Naismith decided.[4]

Naismith's game was an instant hit with his class, who did not care that they had to climb up and remove the ball from the basket whenever a point was scored. They took the idea home with them on Christmas vacation and taught their friends to play. When they returned, they organized

The All-American Red Heads

The All American Red Heads were one of the first professional women's basketball teams in the United States. They were established in 1936, played until 1986, and were surpassed only by the Harlem Globetrotters as a barnstorming attraction.

The Red Heads were founded by C. M. "Ole" Olson, and their name was inspired by Olson's wife, who owned a number of beauty salons. Players who did not naturally have red hair used a vegetable dye called henna to color it.

Fans throughout the years loved the Red Heads partly because of their skillful play that included trick shots like dribbling with the knees, and partly because they played so well. During their first decade on the road, they claimed a victory rate of more than 50 percent against male opponents. In later years they did even better. Orwell Moore, who began coaching them in 1948 stated, "I would say that from 1950 to 1975 we probably won 85 or 90 percent of the time."

Quoted in Robert R. Peterson, *Cages to Jump Shots*. New York: Oxford University Press, 1990, p. 104.

teams to play against each other during the noon hour. Spectators began gathering on the balcony to watch the enthusiastic competitions. Naismith was asked to make copies of the rules, and they were soon published in the school newspaper.

As word of the game got around, physical education teacher Senda Berenson introduced it to her students at Smith College for women in nearby Northampton. Her first teams hit the court in 1892. The game caught on and quickly spread from Smith to other women's colleges across the country. Many people were afraid that female basketball players would not be strong enough to play the game, because women were seen as a weaker, inferior sex at the time. That was not the

SLAM DUNK

In 1985, WNBA star Lynette Woodard became the first female Harlem Globetrotter.

case, however. Berenson wrote in 1914, "The game … has been encouraged because by means of it the girls have been made strong and agile in body, keen and fearless in mind, and unselfish and loyal in spirit."[5]

Changes for the Better

As with all new inventions, basketball needed a few changes and improvements to make it work better. Peach baskets were soon replaced with wire and mesh hoops, although the hoops remained closed at the bottom. Open bottom hoops were not introduced until 1914. Backboards were installed

Backboards were added to basketball hoops as a way to prevent the audience from interfering with the basket.

to keep spectators in the balconies from interfering with the basket. Team size was set at five to help with overcrowding on the court. Later, team numbers were expanded to include ten to fifteen players, but a limit of five per team on the court at a given time remained the rule.

New terms such as blocking and charging came into use. Blocking is legally hitting or catching a ball that is being shot toward the basket without touching the opponent's hands. Charging is illegal contact by moving or pushing into an opponent's body. Running with the ball, originally considered a foul, became a violation, meaning that the only penalty was loss of possession. Striking the ball with the fist also became a violation rather than a foul.

Dribbling—controlling or advancing the ball by bouncing it—was introduced early in the game, but just as quickly became a cause for dispute. Naismith's rules stated that the ball had to be thrown from the place where it was caught. Ingenious players tried to get around this, however, with moves such as tapping the ball into the air, taking a step and then catching it. Some rolled it, ran after it, and picked it up. Others simply bounced it. Such moves were frowned on by traditionalists, but dribbling continued and was quickly accepted in women's and collegiate games. Finally, in 1929 dribbling was made legal, and players began to develop such impressive plays as the "behind the back," the "crossover," and the "half-reverse" dribble. In the crossover, the player dribbles one-handed, then abruptly changes hands and dribbles one-handed in another direction. In the half-reverse, the player turns, pretending to be reversing direction, then turns back, and dribbles in the original direction.

The Barnstorming Era

Basketball was first introduced and played in YMCAs, and thus many YMCA teams were the first to turn professional and charge spectators to watch their games. One of the first professional teams was the Trentons of New Jersey, who reportedly earned $15 each in their first contest against the Brooklyn YMCA on November 7, 1896. The game drew a crowd of 700 spectators.

In 1897 twelve amateur teams met to take part in the Amateur Athletic Unions' first national basketball championship tournament. After winning the tournament, the Twenty-Third Street YMCA team decided to go professional and was instantly kicked out of their home Y. Sports professionals had a bad reputation at the time. Early physical education instructor Luther Gulick wrote, "When men commence to make money out of sport, it degenerates with most tremendous speed. ... It has in the past inevitably resulted in men of lower character going into the game."[6]

Without a home court, the Twenty-third Street team changed its name to the New York Wanderers and gained fame as the first basketball barnstormers. The term *barnstormer* was initially used to describe stunt pilots who traveled to rural parts of the country, landed at local farms, and put on air shows for area residents. Basketball barnstormers like the Wanderers, the Troy Trojans, and the Oswego Indians toured small and large towns by bus and train, played one or two games for pay, and then moved on. They had no contracts and no guarantees. Pay was so low that many players had to work at other jobs to survive. Some played for more than one team at a time. Their schedule involved hours of travel interrupted by hotly contested games in school gyms, armories (military structures), and meeting halls.

Black Fives

By the 1920s there were hundreds of men's professional basketball teams. All were independent, and like the rest of American society at the time, all were segregated by race. Nevertheless, dozens of talented African American men played on amateur and pro teams sponsored by black churches, social clubs, businesses, colleges, and YMCAs. Such all-black teams were known as "Black Fives," for the number of players per team.

Two Black Five barnstorming teams—the New York Renaissance, also known as the Harlem Rens, and the Harlem Globetrotters—quickly made names for themselves as the best in the business. The Rens played for more than twenty-five years and had a win-loss record of 2,318 to 381.

Many of their wins were against top all-white teams, such as the Original Celtics. The Globetrotters, originally known as the Savoy Big Five, began barnstorming in 1927, played 175 games a year, and won more than 90 percent of them. By 1949, thanks to their fancy ball-handling and trick shooting, they were basketball's biggest attraction.

Despite both teams' immense popularity, their travel schedules were regularly complicated by the fact that they were not welcome in most restaurants and hotels. Promoter Sidney Goldman recalled of his team, the Toledo Jim White Chevrolets: "The blacks had to sleep in the car. It was cold, and I remember taking the uniforms out and putting them in the car to use for blankets. I had a room, but I felt guilty so I went out and slept in the car with them."[7]

Chuck Cooper was the first African American to be drafted by the National Basketball Association (NBA).

Beginning in the late 1940s, integration began to change basketball. In 1950 Chuck Cooper became the first African American drafted by the National Basketball Association (NBA), North America's premier league for professionals. By the 1960s African -Americans were highly visible on both college and professional levels. In 1964 the Boston Celtics had an all-black starting lineup. The percentage of black players continued to grow throughout the years until by the 2008–2009 season, more than 80 percent of all NBA players were black.

College Teams and the NCAA

At the same time that professional basketball developed, high school and college teams flourished as well. Only a few good players were needed to make a team, so even small schools could be competitive and could draw attention to themselves through the sport.

The first official intercollegiate game was played in January 1896, when the University of Chicago defeated the University of Iowa by a score of 15 to 12. The National College Athletic Association (NCAA) was created and sponsored its first national tournament in 1939, but the large number of college leagues that developed were regional. They did not draw a national audience until the advent of television in the 1950s.

The rise of a remarkable group of college athletes in the 1950s and 1960s helped college basketball gain in popularity. Players like Elgin Baylor, Oscar Robertson, Jerry West, Wilt Chamberlain, and Bill Russell became stars, defying earlier basketball customs and initiating new plays such as the head fake, the running bank shot, and the fade away jump shot. The head fake involves moving the head to make it look like a player is going in one direction, then actually moving in another direction. A running bank shot is a shot made when a running player bounces the ball off the backboard and into the basket. The fade away jump shot is a shot taken while the player is jumping backwards away from the basket. Fans were amazed by their heroes' size and agility. Baylor and Robertson were 6 foot 5 inches (195.6 cm), Russell was 6 foot 10 inches (208.3 cm), and Chamberlain was 7 foot 1 inch (215.9 cm). When those men went on to become professional players, other exceptional college athletes took their place. Teams like the UCLA Bruins (University of California Los Angeles), the North Carolina Tar Heels (University of North Carolina), the Kentucky Wildcats (University of Kentucky), and the Indiana Hoosiers (Indiana University) became known for producing star players such as Kareem Abdul-Jabbar, Larry Bird, and the legendary Michael Jordan.

Professionals Associations

From the 1960s on, most college basketball stars turned professional before or immediately after leaving school. When it was founded in 1949, the NBA promoted and regulated

Despite receiving less publicity than men's basketball, the Women's National Basketball Association (WNBA) players— like Tamika Catchings—have produced a vast fan following.

seventeen professional basketball teams that were members. In 2010 the association was composed of thirty teams. The NBA-backed Women's National Basketball Association (WNBA) began in 1996 and is made up of twelve teams. Although less publicized than men's basketball, WNBA players such as Lynette Woodard, Tina Thompson, and Tamika Catchings have generated enormous fan loyalty. Sportswriter

GAME ATTENDANCE: PAST AND PRESENT

Boston Celtics Attendance, 1946 to the Present

Season *	Average Fans Per Game
1946-47 thru 1949-50	4,149
1950-51 thru 1959-60	7,575
1960-61 thru 1969-70	8,203
1970-71 thru 1979-80	11,204
1980-81 thru 1989-90	14,881
1990-91 thru 1999-2000	16,071
2000-01 thru 2009-2010	17,009

* Statistics reflect regular season and not playoff attendance

Data acquired from NBA.com, ESPN.com, and APBR.org

Big Men

Tall men are the norm in basketball today, but few men were more than six-feet (182.9 cm) tall in the early days of the game. Teams averaged about five foot ten inches (177.8 cm), with the tallest players no more than six foot two (188 cm). Tall men were considered too clumsy and uncoordinated to play basketball.

Over time taller men joined the game, but they were criticized as "goons" who relied on their size rather than skill. George Mikan, a bespectacled, six foot ten inch (208 cm) newcomer, finally demonstrated that tall men could also be agile, skillful players. "I call him the 'The Original Big Man,'" NBA star Kevin Garnett said. "Without George Mikan, there would be no up-and-unders, no jump hooks, and there would be no label of the big man."

Today, the average height of a professional basketball player is six foot seven inches (200.6 cm). In 2010 Yao Ming of the Houston Rockets at seven foot six inches (228.6 cm) was the tallest player in the NBA.

Quoted in "Mikan Was First Pro to Dominate the Post," *ESPN.com*, June 3, 2005. http://espn.go.com/classic/obit/s/2005/0602/2074322.html.

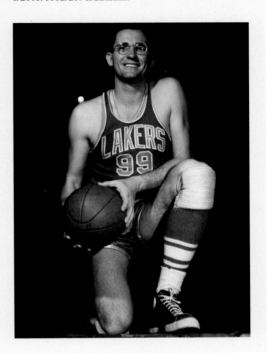

George Mikan was the first "big man" to reveal that tall men could be agile basketball players.

Sally Jenkins says, "We are moving forward by leaps and bounds. We won the Olympic gold medal in 1996, and we got TV ratings. The women's college game is more popular than ever. Unprecedented numbers of girls and women are playing. ... We have arrived."[8]

In the twenty-first century, Naismith's game is played professionally in more than two hundred countries around the world. The International Basketball Federation, founded in

1932 in Geneva, Switzerland, includes a total of 214 national member federations. World championship tournaments for men and women take place every four years, and the champion team wins the Naismith Trophy, named in honor of basketball's creator.

In the United States, basketball is a national passion, with media and the fans unable to get enough of the exploits of players like Ray Allen, Kobe Bryant, Dwayne Wade, and LeBron James. Their public and private lives are constantly in the news, and young players aspire to walk in their shoes. Their popularity has also led the sport to become highly commercialized, with networks and advertisers paying millions to get broadcasting rights, and players signing lucrative contracts in return for their services. Wade and James are two who have multimillion-dollar contracts and earn millions more endorsing everything from mobile phones to bubblegum. Although such costs have also translated to high-ticket prices, fans remain loyal to their favorite players and teams even in tough economic times.

With so much fame and fortune at stake, competition to get to the top in the sport is fierce, and aspiring players and their coaches know that height and natural talent is no longer enough to succeed. Thus, most turn to science to improve their performance. Using discipline, physics, and psychology, they focus on everything from muscles to motivation to master one of the most popular and fast-moving games in the world.

CHAPTER 2

The Discipline of Training

I n the early days of basketball, players received little or no scientific training in the sport. Most relied on time-honored principles of eating well and getting plenty of sleep to stay strong and healthy. They used nothing but their natural athletic abilities to carry out the moves of the game.

Over the years and with scientific progress, everyone discovered that when players followed training plans, kept themselves in peak condition, and worked to perfect their weaknesses, they became stronger, faster, and more agile. By the late twentieth century, training had become serious business. "It's a year round job," says Steven M. Traina, physician for the Denver Nuggets. "Most of our players have been working out together prior to [training] camp, having informal workouts. Guys just don't go fishing and then show up and play basketball."[9]

Healthy Muscles

Players need strength, speed, and agility to play the game well, and that calls for healthy muscles. The human body is made up of three types of muscles—smooth, which make up blood vessels and body organs; cardiac, which make up the walls of the heart; and skeletal, which move and support the skeleton. It is the latter that give athletes strength and

help their bodies move. There are approximately 640 skeletal muscles in the human body. Skeletal muscles are fibers made up of bundles of individual cells called "myocytes." Found within each cell are myofibrils, strands of protein that lengthen and shorten. When they shorten, the muscle contracts (becomes shorter and thicker) and moves the body part it is attached to.

Muscle fibers are also divided into different types, depending on how fast they contract. "Slow twitch" fibers contract slowly, with little force, for long periods of time. "Fast twitch" fibers contract quickly and powerfully, and tire rapidly. Muscles are generally made up of both types of fibers, but some individuals have more of one type than another. Marathon runners, for instance, have up to 80 percent slow twitch fibers, which help them maintain activities for hours on end. The muscles of sprinters, on the other hand, are made up of 80 percent fast twitch fibers.

Sore Muscles

The condition known as "sore muscles" is the pain or discomfort that exercisers often feel 24 to 72 hours after working out too hard or beginning a new exercise program. The scientific name for the condition is Delayed Onset Muscle Soreness (DOMS), and no one is sure exactly what causes it.

For years researchers thought DOMS resulted from increased lactic acid concentrations in the muscles. Studies, however, proved that high levels of lactic acid only lasted about an hour after exercise. Today, many experts believe the pain is a result of microscopic tearing of muscle fibers, brought on by exercise. Others believe DOMS is not caused by damaged muscles, but by the increasing size of muscle fibers that press on nerves and cause temporary pain.

Without a known cause, there is no effective treatment of DOMS. Gentle stretching, warming up, and cooling down before and after exercise may reduce it. Ultimately, the best advice for treating DOMS is preventing it in the first place.

Basketball is a game that requires both endurance and bursts of energy, so players work to develop both their fast and slow twitch abilities. To develop fast twitch fibers, they practice jumping or sprinting. For slow twitch fibers, they do endurance workouts. They swim or tread water, jog, or lift relatively light hand weights for long periods of time.

Building Speed, Strength, and Agility

To be fast on the court, players need fast twitch muscles that are well developed. To work on speed, they practice sprints and speed drills, such as line jumps (jumping quickly back and forth over a line), running backward, or jumping rope rapidly.

SLAM DUNK

42

Percent of the average adult male body mass that is muscle; 36 percent of the average adult female body mass is muscle.

Strength is also essential for players when they jump, throw, and guard other players. The more often their muscles contract against resistance, the stronger they get. Players build strength by using exercise equipment such as hand weights, bench presses, and medicine balls. They repeat sets of squats, lunges, bicep curls, and push-ups. No muscle group is overlooked. Dribbling, for instance, requires a great deal of finger and wrist strength, so players work this specific area by doing forearm curls with a pair of hand weights. "People used to think in basketball that if you lifted weights, you couldn't shoot because you'd be too muscle-bound," says Traina. "[Players] spend a lot of time in the weight room. You look at the athletes now compared to 20 or 25 years ago, and they're cut, they're muscular."[10]

Players also need agility, which is the ability to move quickly, smoothly, and coordinately. To improve agility, players focus on drills that involve rapid weaving, sprinting, and shuffling in complex pre-set patterns. They do hurdle drills where they have to run over mini hurdles. They do snake drills where they sprint around cones set in staggered patterns. They do side-to-side jumping drills to help with lateral (sideways) mobility.

Muscle Memory

Agility is best when movements are performed instinctively. To make basketball moves automatic, players work to develop muscle memory. Muscle memory is the ability of the brain to remember and direct the body to carry out often-repeated muscle moves without conscious thinking.

Shooting a basketball involves muscle memory. Coach Brad Winters says, "Like practically everything else in life, basketball shooting is a habitual thing; that is, it involves repetition of a given set of movements until those movements become an unconscious part of a player's court behavior."[11] Other moves that involve muscle memory include the "show and go" move where a player pretends to dodge to one side, then darts immediately in the opposite

SLAM DUNK

Gluteus maximus

The biggest (bulkiest) skeletal muscle in the human body.

direction, and the "crossover," where the player bounces a ball at a 45-degree angle from one hand to the other without looking at it.

The average player must repeat a move correctly about twenty thousand times to make it automatic. Because basketball players are always carrying out moves they would not ordinarily do in life, such as running backward, gliding while changing direction, and so forth, they have to practice hundreds of hours until moves are second nature. NBA All-Star Bill Russell, renowned for his defense and shot-blocking skills, stated, "Every move has six or seven years of work behind it."[12]

When players shoot the basketball, they are using their muscle memory.

Explosive Power

Basketball players need bursts of power to make powerful jump shots, rebounds, passes, and other moves. Plyometric drills, designed to build fast, explosive movements, help them prepare for that. Plyometrics is a type of training that improves the function of the nervous system. Repeated drills condition nerves to contract with a single vigorous surge, causing a fast, powerful contraction of muscles. The concept was developed in the 1960s by Soviet scientist Yuri Verkhoshansky, who called it "shock training." U.S. track and field coach Fred Wilt coined the word "plyometrics" in 1975.

Plyometrics drills are fast and strenuous. For example, during "clap push-ups," players get into a push-up position. They then repeatedly push up, clap their hands together, then quickly put their hands down to catch themselves. In "power skips" players drive their knees forcefully upward as they skip forward. Arm action is a forceful, exaggerated running motion.

Because of their emphasis on speed and power, plyometrics drills can cause muscle damage if they are not done correctly.

A Handy Advantage

Ambidexterity is the ability to use either hand with ease for different activities, and it is unusual in everyday life. Most people are right-handed. That means they are more skillful using their right hand than their left. Studies suggest that 70 to 90 percent of the world's population is right-handed.

Ambidexterity is a skill that is an asset in basketball, however. Players who can use both their right and left hands for dribbling and shooting have a definite advantage over single-hand-dominant players. Therefore, many players train themselves with hours of practice to be able to use either hand. Such has been the case with players Michael Jordan, LeBron James, and Kobe Bryant. Forwards Michael Beasley of the Miami Heat and Candace Parker of the Los Angeles Sparks are both naturally ambidextrous.

Los Angeles Sparks' Candace Parker displays her ambidexterity.

If muscles are not strong enough they cannot support the explosive extensions and contractions that take place. Incorrect use of plyometric training has also been linked with various forms of chronic injuries such as heel pad bruising, shin splints, and stress fractures of the foot. Juan Carlos Santana, director of the Institute of Human Performance, cautions, "Like any other high-risk maneuver, high intensity plyometrics should not be designed or performed without the supervision of a professional overseeing the training."[13]

Training Wisely

The likelihood of suffering an injury during the game can be lessened if players follow a proper training program. This concept is called "prehibilitation." Sports expert and coach Raphael Brandon explains, "The concept of 'prehabilitation' exercise training is now becoming well-known with trainers and therapists. ... Prehabilitation involves strength and conditioning exercises for specific muscles that help to reduce injury risks, before an injury actually occurs. It's the classic 'an ounce of prevention is better than a pound of cure' approach to physical training."[14]

Ironically, some injuries occur during training because players do not train correctly. For instance, they train too often and/or too hard. They may change from one sport to another without proper conditioning for the new sport. These situations often take place at the beginning of the season when players return from vacations and plunge enthusiastically into a new routine. Training injuries also occur if players neglect warm-ups and flexibility exercises. Warm-ups such as jogging or calisthenics increase muscle temperature and allow for better stretching. Stretching and flexibility exercises develop a greater range of motion of the joints, which lessens the risk of tears, strains, or falls.

Despite the risk of training injuries, following a proper training program generally results in fewer injuries during the season. Strong muscles are able to support bones and joints better. Proper alignment (positioning) of shoulders, hips, and feet helps joints and muscles move more freely with less stress and strain. Sharp reflexes allow for more coordinated movements. Basketball coach and author Alan Stein explains, "In order to reduce the occurrence of injury in your program, you should have your players participate in a comprehensive year-round training program. This includes having them warm up … before every workout, perform strength training and pre-hab exercises, limit the overuse of plyometrics … and give them ample rest to recover."[15]

Year-Round Training

Some level of year-round training is the norm in basketball, but players are most highly motivated to get into shape during the preseason. That begins the month before the start of a new season. During the preseason, athletes undergo intense training. They work hard on their drills and their running, and also spend time working on their weaknesses. Knicks assistant coach Herb Williams says, "We keep tabs on all the guys' individual workouts, making sure they stay in shape and do what they got to do. It's just about getting ready for the season."[16]

Once the season begins, players work full time putting all their training into practice during games. The intensity lessens during postseason, except for those winning teams who enter the playoffs.

Off-season is the time when there is no official competition. This is when players recover from any injuries they suffered during the season. Many also take this opportunity to play another sport such as baseball or tennis. Others maintain general fitness by hiking, biking, jogging, or swimming two to three times a week. Some professionals join summer leagues affiliated with the NBA. Two such leagues are the Orlando Pro Summer League, run by the Orlando Magic, and the NBA Summer League in Las Vegas, run by the NBA. Teams usually consist of players who have been in the league for three years or less, as well as newly drafted talent. "NBA Summer League provides incoming rookies an opportunity to begin the acclimation [adjustment] process to the NBA while [providing] further training for veteran players,"[17] says Stu Jackson, executive vice president of NBA Basketball Operations.

Sports Nutrition

The off-season is the opportunity for athletes to enjoy some of their favorite foods and drinks, because, when they are in training, they know that they need to carefully monitor what they eat. During that time they want their body systems to be working well to reach their highest potential. The best way to achieve this is to eat a variety of nutritious foods that includes fruits, vegetables, lean meats, and whole grains. All are vital to provide the strength and energy needed to play basketball.

Just because they monitor their diet does not mean they go hungry, however. In contrast to the average person who needs about 2,000 calories per day to carry out routine tasks, a seven-foot tall male basketball player may need up to 7,000 calories per day. A calorie is a measure of the energy found in food. The average piece of bread has about 100 calories. One chicken nugget has about 50 calories. A piece of chocolate cake has more than 200 calories.

Proper Nutrition

Basketball players in training eat a diet high in carbohydrates and low in fats, simple sugars, and alcohol. The following is a sample menu that would provide one day's nutritional requirements for a professional adult player.

Breakfast: Glass of orange juice, large bowl of raisin bran cereal, and a banana.
Snack: One cup of yogurt and two granola bars.
Lunch: Two turkey sandwiches, an apple, milk, and four oatmeal cookies.
Snack: Two peanut butter and jelly sandwiches and milk.
Dinner: Two chicken breasts, potatoes, steamed vegetables, and a roll.
Snack: Two English muffins with peanut butter.

Alan Stein, "Nutritional Guide for Basketball Players." *Powerbasketball.com*, 1998. www.powerbasketball.com/071027.html.

No matter how many calories players consume, their training diet should be approximately 60 to 65 percent carbohydrates, 15 to 20 percent fat, and 10 to 15 percent protein. Carbohydrates provide fuel needed for physical activity and are found in whole grains, fruits, vegetables, beans, and potatoes. Alcohol and simple sugars such as those found in candy and soda are also carbohydrates, but these do not contribute to good health, so athletes should eat them sparingly. Proteins are building blocks

To maintain body systems it is important for players to keep hydrated with water or sports drinks.

needed to make muscle, bone, hair, and virtually every other body tissue. They are part of enzymes, which power many chemical reactions, and hemoglobin, which carries oxygen in the blood. The body cannot store protein, so players need to eat .02 to .03 ounces (.6 to .8 gm) of lean meat, fish, cheese, nuts, or soy protein per pound of body weight per day. Fats should be limited to heart healthy oils like canola or olive oil.

Drinking plenty of water or sports drinks is also vital for players to maintain body systems. Fluid is important for regulating temperature through sweating, elimination of waste products, and facilitating digestion, and even a loss of 2 percent of one's body weight through sweating can cause a drop in blood volume. When that happens, the heart has to work harder to move blood through the bloodstream, and players may experience muscle cramps, dizziness, fatigue, or even heat exhaustion or heat stroke.

Supplements and Substance Abuse

When training and good nutrition is not enough, some basketball players turn to supplements to improve their performance on the court. A few supplements such as high-protein drinks are considered acceptable within sports associations, because they are made of naturally occurring ingredients. Creatine, a non-steroid that allegedly builds muscles and generates energy, is also legal and popular, but it is frowned upon by many, including the NCAA, because its safety has not been proven. It also gives athletes who use it an unfair advantage over those who do not.

Many performance-enhancing substances are banned by all sports organizations in the United States. These include stimulants such as cocaine, narcotics like heroin and morphine, cannabinoids such as marijuana, and hormones such as human growth hormone and anabolic steroids. Anabolic steroids are synthetically produced variants of the male hormone testosterone. Like testosterone, they increase muscle size and strength and improve a player's stamina.

Few documented cases exist of the abuse of banned substances, particularly anabolic steroids, among college

POSSIBLE SIDE EFFECTS OF ANABOLIC STEROID USE

Dizziness

Oily hair

Hair loss

Acne

Bad breath

Nausea and vomiting

Stunted growth

Increased risk of heart disease, stroke, and some cancers

Various sexual side affects

Liver damage

Aching joints

Increased risk of muscle injury

Trembling

High blood pressure

Insomnia

Increased risk of muscle injury

Mood swings, paranoia, delusions

Particular to girls
• Growth of facial hair   • Menstrual cycle changes

Adapted from http://kidshealth.org/teen/food_fitness/sports/steroids.html#:

and professional basketball players. Some believe that this is because the NBA's testing is lax, although the organization disputes that. NBA commissioner David Stern says, "I believe that the NBA's current anti-drug program is strong, effective, and appropriate for our sport, and remains committed to ensuring that it remains state-of-the-art."[18]

Playing It Smart

Many believe the NBA is doing enough; they argue that basketball players are unlikely to use steroids because they do not want to pack on weight and muscles. Instead they want to be lean, agile, and quick. Still, there are banned substances other than steroids, and a number of players have been caught and fined for using them. In 2006 New Orleans Hornets forward Chris Andersen was dismissed from the NBA for

After being dismissed for testing positive for a banned substance, Chris Andersen was reinstated to the NBA in 2008.

testing positive for an undisclosed banned substance. He was reinstated in 2008. In 2009 Orlando Magic forward Rashad Lewis was suspended for ten games after testing positive for dehydroepiandrosterone (DHEA), a banned compound found in some health food supplements. He accepted the suspension, but insisted he had not knowingly broken the rule. "I think the league knows I made an honest mistake," he says. "They worked with me closely on this. It just lets you know that you can't just go to a Walgreens Drug Store and pick up vitamins if you don't know what's in them. I don't take anything now except water."[19]

Substance abuse is potentially a more serious problem among teen basketball players who are just getting into the game and think that steroids will help them qualify for sports scholarships or professional careers. No one knows the numbers, but according to the National Institute on Drug Abuse, 2.2 percent of 12th graders surveyed in 2008 confirmed that they had used steroids in their lifetime. This is despite the fact that steroids can have serious side effects such as high blood pressure, liver damage, and stunted growth. Gary Wadler, professor at New York University School of Medicine, explains, "What happens is that steroids close the growth centers in a kid's bones. Once these growth plates are closed, they cannot reopen so adolescents that take too many steroids may end up shorter than they should have been."[20]

With so many disadvantages, experts believe that everyone from teens to professionals should realize that they can become great athletes without drugs. Family Education.com emphasizes, "Sports should be about learning persistence and dedication, and the value of working hard to reach a goal. People who take shortcuts to get there don't just cheat the competition—they cheat themselves."[21]

CHAPTER 3

Sports Medicine

Despite the training and proper nutrition basketball players emphasize, they still sometimes get injured when they play. This is not surprising considering that their light uniforms provide little protection. Their joints and muscles pull and twist as they pivot, leap, and sprint around the court. They crash into each other and fall. Author Dan Bell writes, "The physically demanding nature of NBA basketball requires a fine-tuned body capable of surviving 82-plus games each year. But bumps, bruises and, unfortunately, injuries are always a part of each season. Staying healthy and, where necessary, coming back as quickly as possible from an injury, are vital to any team's success."[22]

Breaks and Bruises

Basketball injuries fall into two general categories: acute and chronic. Chronic injuries develop over time, whereas acute injuries are caused by specific events such as high impact blows, heavy falls, or unnatural movements. Depending on how serious the acute injury, such events can lead to pain, swelling, dislocated joints, broken bones, or even loss of consciousness.

Broken bones are some of the most common acute injuries. A break can be as simple as a crack or as complicated as a compound fracture, in which the bone is completely broken and punctures the skin. Depending on the severity

Who Gets Hurt?

Although basketball is not considered as rough as football, it creates a huge number of injuries, as the following statistics, compiled by the British Columbia Injury Research and Prevention Unit, demonstrate.

- Each year more than 1.6 million basketball-related injuries are treated in hospitals, doctor's offices, and emergency rooms in North America. Of those injuries, 574,000 involve children ages five to fourteen years.
- All players in all positions are at risk of suffering injuries.
- For elementary children in Physical Education (PE) class, 20 percent of injuries occur while playing basketball.
- One out of every four basketball players, both male and female, at the high school level has suffered at least one injury per year that results in time lost from play or practice.
- Males ages fifteen to nineteen have the highest injury rate, whereas females ages ten to fourteen are the most frequently injured.
- The overall injury rate is slightly higher for females than for males, with females having more severe injuries and more injuries requiring surgery.

"Basketball Injuries," *BC Injury Research and Prevention Unit*, 2006. www.injuryresearch.bc.ca/Publications/Fact%20Sheets/basketball%20fact%20sheet.pdf.

SLAM DUNK

Landing on the balls of your feet, rather than flat-footed, may help prevent ACL injuries.

and location of the break, team doctors sometimes use splints and tape to brace and protect the injury to allow a player to participate. In other cases the player must sit out of the game for a few weeks until the break has time to heal.

Another common acute injury is the contusion, commonly called a bruise. A bruise is an area where small blood vessels known as capillaries have been

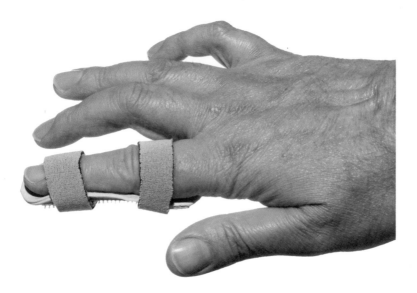

Team doctors occasionally use tape and splints to protect a broken bone while allowing a player to continue in the basketball game.

damaged, allowing blood to leak and accumulate in the surrounding tissue. The build-up causes the reddish-purple marks that everyone recognizes. Although most bruises are not severe, some can be dangerous. A hard blow that bruises an organ such as the heart can cause permanent damage. Bruises to the brain can lead to swelling, concussion, coma, and death.

Strains and Sprains

The strain and the sprain are two other common acute injuries. Strains involve stretched or torn tendons, the tissue that connects muscles to bones. They can occur anywhere, but are most common in the back, the hamstrings (tendons at the rear of the knee), and the elbows. Sprains occur when ligaments, the tough fibrous tissue that connect bones to other bones, are overstretched or torn.

Because players are always making sharp turns and twists, sprained ankles are the most common type of sprain in basketball. Most sprained ankles are lateral sprains involving the anterior talofibular ligament on the outside of the ankle. Players do damage when the ankle rolls onto the outside part of the foot.

A high ankle sprain is rarer, but more serious, than a lateral sprain. High sprains often occur when the foot is forced

There are three basic types of ankle sprains: lateral inversions (the ankle rolls outward), lateral eversion (the ankle rolls inward), and high sprains (the leg twists while the foot stays planted). Each sprain involves painful torn ligaments and can mean months of recovery for injured athletes.

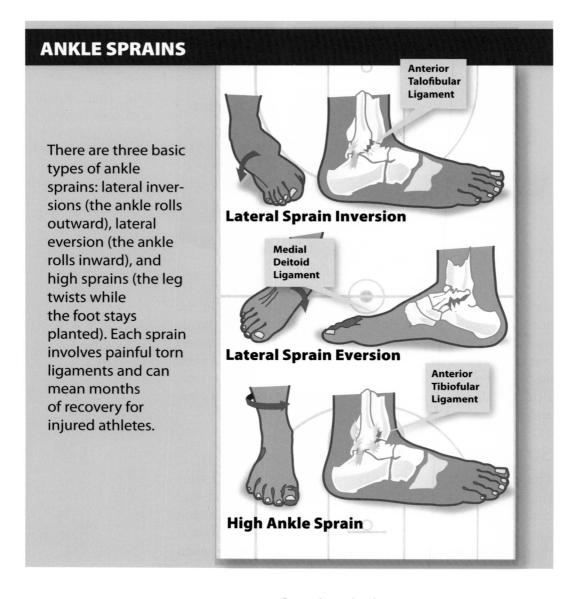

Anterior Talofibular Ligament

Lateral Sprain Inversion

Medial Deitoid Ligament

Lateral Sprain Eversion

Anterior Tibiofular Ligament

High Ankle Sprain

to rotate outward or when the foot cannot move and the leg is twisted. Damage is done to the syndesmotic ligaments, which lie above the ankle joint and wrap around the lower end of the shinbones. When these ligaments tear, the two bones may separate when a player puts weight on the foot. The injury results in an unstable ankle, which is extremely painful. The patient may have to wear a cast and take up to six months to recover.

"My Finger Just Popped Out"

Dislocations are another type of acute injury common to basketball. In a dislocation a force moves bones from their normal position in a joint. Bones are commonly held in place by ligaments, tendons, and muscles, so these are all injured during a dislocation.

Finger joints are delicate and easily dislocated by a fall or other impact. The most common finger dislocations occur in the middle knuckle of fingers. In January 2009 LA Lakers'

Dislocations, like the dislocated finger LA Lakers' Kobe Bryant suffered, are an acute injury.

Kobe Bryant dislocated his ring finger while grabbing the ball. "I just dove for the ball, and [my] finger just popped out,"[23] he recalled.

Shoulders can dislocate, too, when a hard impact causes the rounded head of the upper arm bone to pop out of the socket. Dislocations are relatively easy to fix by manipulating the joint until the two bones are properly aligned, but rest and protection of the injured area are necessary for full recovery.

Damaged Knees

Players sometimes downplay sprains and dislocations, but when it comes to knees, they take injuries more seriously. The knee is the largest and most complicated joint in the body. It is a pivotal hinge point where the end of the thighbone meets the top of the shinbone. Four main ligaments connect these bones. The medial collateral ligament (MCL) runs along the inner part of the knee, preventing it from bending inward. The lateral collateral ligament (LCL) runs along the outer part of the knee, preventing it from bending outward. The anterior cruciate ligament (ACL) lies in the middle of the knee and prevents the shinbone from sliding out in front of the thighbone. It stabilizes the knee. The posterior cruciate ligament (PCL) prevents the shinbone from sliding backward under the thighbone.

PCL injuries usually occur when the knee is struck from the front and/or hyper-extended. ACL injuries commonly occur when an athlete changes direction rapidly, twists without moving the feet, or stumbles and falls. Because of the complexity of the knee joint, these injuries can become game-ending events because torn ligaments generally require surgery to repair. In February 2009, for instance, Minnesota Timberwolf Al Jefferson tore the ACL in his right knee when he landed hard, so he was out the rest of the season.

Knee injuries are not only serious, they are frequent, especially among female athletes who have a rate of ACL injuries two to eight times higher than males. Twelve of the eighteen top players on the 1996 U.S. Olympic women's basketball team have had ACL problems. Experts believe this may be because, compared to men, women have wider hips and looser ligaments due to hormone fluctuations. Both can affect knee movements. Trainer Laura Ramus of the Detroit Shocks says, "If they have to stop quickly and turn, then it's more likely they're injured."[24]

Head Injury

In both men and women, the head is another part of the body that is at high risk for serious injury. The most common acute injury to the head is the concussion. A concussion is usually caused when a player hits or is hit by something, whether a hard surface or another player. As a result of the blow, soft brain tissue bounces against the hard inner surface of the skull, causing bruising, bleeding, and/or tearing of nerve fibers.

A concussion—the most common acute injury—can cause a player to experience dizziness, sleepiness, confusion, nausea, and a headache.

   Most people with concussions do not lose consciousness, but they may experience symptoms that include confusion, headache, dizziness, nausea, and sleepiness. Such symptoms

Repeated Concussions

Doctors know that repeated concussions put athletes at risk for later problems such as long-term memory loss and Alzheimer's disease. Thus, they are concerned with the rising number of head injuries on the court. No known studies track concussions in basketball players, but in January 2009 alone, NBA players Marvin Williams of the Atlanta Hawks, Brian Scalabrine of the Boston Celtics, and Trevor Ariza of the Houston Rockets all left games or practices because of concussions. Scalabrine sustained two during that period. Del Harris, who has been an NBA coach since 1976, says, "I don't know if guys had harder heads or if we didn't jump as high. Either one is possible. But there was not the kind of frequency that we've been having lately with that."

To help protect against concussions, some players are using specially designed mouth protectors that position the jaw to cushion the shock of some blows. The value of such mouth protectors is still being debated, but there is no debate that allowing players to suffer repeated concussions is a practice that needs to change.

Houston Rockets' Trevor Ariza has sustained a concussion. Repeated concussions put athletes at risk for memory loss and Alzheimer's disease.

Quoted in Scott Howard-Cooper, "NBA Sees Sudden, Scary Increase in Concussions," *The Sacramento Bee*, February 25, 2009, p. 1C. http://neurosurgery.ucla.edu/work-files/In%20the%20news/Hovda%5B1%5D.Sac.Bee.pdf.

commonly disappear on their own, and many athletes fail to report them if they are mild. If symptoms continue or include convulsions, muscle weakness, vision problems, or unconsciousness, however, hospitalization and emergency treatment is warranted.

Studies show that the risk of a getting another concussion rises after a player suffers a first, and damage from several concussions increases the risk of mental disorders, long-term memory loss, and Alzheimer's disease. Females and young athletes appear to be at higher risk for concussions than male players. It is unclear why this is so, but experts guess that it is partly because their necks are smaller and less muscular than adult males' necks and thus provide less stability. Pediatric emergency medicine specialist Jean Ogborn says, "Concussions occur in girls' sports with significant frequency, and … girls and their parents need to be aware that these injuries must be carefully managed to prevent permanent damage."[25] Knowledgeable coaches know that players should not go back into a game for at least a week after a concussion to minimize further damage to the brain.

Chronic Injuries

Although sprains, bruises, and concussions are examples of acute injuries, blisters and shin splints (sore muscles along the shinbone in the front lower legs) are examples of common chronic ones. Chronic injuries are usually the result of overuse. They do not immediately put a player out of action, because they can take weeks or months to develop. Still, they can be extremely painful if left untreated. Early symptoms include swelling, a dull ache while a player is resting, and pain while performing activities.

Patellar tendonitis, also known as jumper's knee, is a more serious chronic injury that is caused when microscopic tears occur in the patellar tendon that connects the kneecap to the shinbone. The problem develops as a result of the repeated explosive extensions of the leg that occur when basketball players jump.

Another potentially serious chronic injury is Achilles tendonitis which involves inflammation of the Achilles tendon, the large tendon that connects the heel to the back leg muscles. The Achilles tendon is necessary for walking and standing on tiptoe, and its inflammation makes walking painful and sometimes impossible. It occurs when players, particularly older players whose tendons are less flexible, overwork their feet. If left untreated, the inflammation can create a rupture of the tendon, which then requires surgery.

Stress Fractures

Another common and often serious type of chronic injury is the stress fracture. Stress fractures often occur in the ribs or foot bones, and the damage done is similar to what happens

An often serious chronic injury called a stress fracture, sidelined Houston Rockets' Yao Ming in 2008 and 2009.

to a piece of wood when it is bent back and forth too many times. At a weak spot, a crack finally occurs. Stress fractures can result from improper training or from overworking the body part.

They can also be a consequence of the extreme height and weight of today's college and professional players. Denver Nuggets strength and conditioning coach Steve Hess says, "When you are 7 feet, 270 pounds [213.2 cm, 122.4 kg], the force on that joint is a lot different than a guy 5 feet [152.4 cm]."[26] In both 2008 and 2009, 7 foot 6 inch (228.6 cm) Yao Ming of the Houston Rockets was sidelined with stress fractures of his left foot. "Because of his size.... and what he does playing basketball at his size, he is always at risk of something like this happening," says team physician Tom Clanton.[27]

Despite Yao's difficulties, stress fractures occur less frequently in males, who have larger, denser bones than women. Young people of both sexes whose bones have not reached peak density, however, are also at greater risk. There are no quick fixes for stress fractures. Once they occur, the best treatment is to avoid putting weight on the injury until it heals.

Diagnosis

When sports injuries occur, it is important that they be properly identified and diagnosed. Doctors use several procedures to see what has happened inside the body. The most standard involves X-rays, which are similar to light rays but are of shorter wavelength and can penetrate solids. X-ray machines are the first line of diagnosis for fractures. When the rays meet bone, the bone creates a white shadow on film where the rays cannot get through to the film on the other side of the body. Where there are breaks or fractures, the rays pass through and show as darker lines.

Another standard diagnostic procedure is the computerized tomography scan (CT scan), which was developed in 1970. Tomograms are multiple X-rays taken at different angles and at different levels of the body. CT scans provide three-dimensional images of an injury when an X-ray machine cannot.

How MRIs Work

Magnetic Resonance Imaging (MRI) machines use powerful magnets and radio waves to obtain images of the body. They work because the human body is composed primarily of fat and water, both of which contain hydrogen atoms. In fact, the human body is approximately 63 percent hydrogen atoms.

The magnetic field created by the MRI machine forces hydrogen atoms in the body to line up in a way similar to how the needle on a compass moves when it is held near a magnet. When radio waves are sent toward the lined-up hydrogen atoms, they bounce back, and a computer records the signal. Different types of tissues send back different signals. Healthy tissue sends back a different signal than cancerous tissue, for instance, and experts who are trained to read the results of the procedure are then able to diagnose problems that exist.

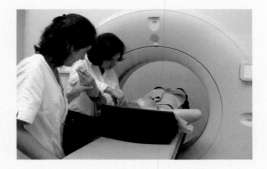

MRI machines acquire images of the body through radio waves and magnets.

Magnetic Resonance Imaging (MRI) is the most recent addition to diagnostic procedures. Introduced in 1977, it does not use radiation, but instead relies on powerful magnets, radio waves, and a computer to collect hundreds of detailed images of both hard and soft tissue. The MRI scans the injury point by point, creating a precise three-dimensional map of tissue types. It can detect abnormalities as tiny as .0008 square inches (.5 square millimeters).

First Aid

Once an injury is diagnosed, it must be properly treated. Treatment can include everything from ice to arthroscopic surgery. Howard J. Luks, chief of sports medicine and arthroscopy at the Westchester Medical Center in New York says, "Techniques are developing literally by the month in sports medicine. They will provide ways to treat problems that were not treatable before, or only treatable through traditional surgery."[28]

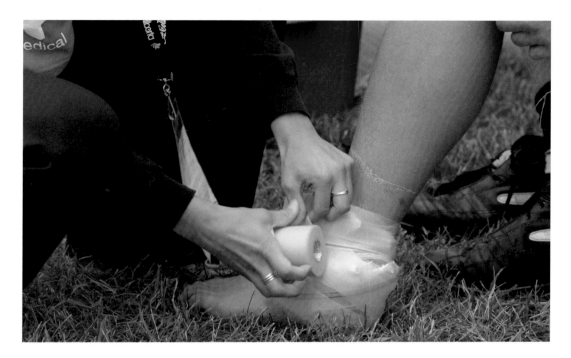

When it comes to acute injuries such as bruises, sprains, and strains; doctors, coaches, and players follow the acronym P.R.I.C.E.—protection, rest, ice, compression, and elevation. Protection with a splint or bandage shields the injury from further damage. Rest allows the damaged muscle, tendon, or ligament to heal. Ice, compression, and elevating the injury above the level of the heart limit swelling. Ice bags or cold packs also decrease the tissue's need for oxygen and preserve muscles cells, while the anesthetic effect of the cold helps to ease pain. Compression, wrapping the injury with a bandage, provides additional stabilization.

Antiflammatory and pain-relieving medicines are another first line of treatment. In the case of acute injuries, athletes can immediately take nonsteroidal drugs such as aspirin, ibuprofen, and naproxen to reduce inflammation and pain. Corticosteroids—hormones such as cortisone, hydrocortisone, prednisone, and others produced by the adrenal glands or synthetically made—are also used to treat chronic soft-tissue injuries. Corticosteroids are commonly injected at the site of pain, but must be used sparingly, because they suppress the immune system and cause other side effects.

Acute injuries such as sprains, bruises, and strains are often treated by following the acronym P.R.I.C.E.— protection, rest, ice, compression, and elevation.

Therapeutic Ultrasound

Some question the value of therapeutic ultrasound, but sports therapists and trainers regularly use it to provide healing in the case of serious bruising, spraining, or straining. They also use it to treat both chronic and acute muscular-skeletal injuries as well as back and joint conditions.

Ultrasound machines work by generating high-frequency sound waves that pass into the skin and vibrate the tissues. The vibration produces heat, which cannot be felt by the patient, but stimulates healing.

Experts guess that ultrasound promotes healing in other ways, too. They think that the waves may attract mast cells (cells involved in healing) to the injury site. Ultrasound may also stimulate the production of collagen, the main protein component in tendons and ligaments, which is necessary in the healing process.

The Last Resort

Sometimes an injury does not respond to first aid or ultrasound. It may be so serious that it must be surgically repaired. Torn cartilage and stress fractures are just two sports injuries that often need surgery before they can heal completely.

Surgery has always been a last resort in sports, because players can miss an entire season while recovering. The latest techniques, such as endoscopic procedures, however, speed up surgery and recovery time. Doctors often do these on an outpatient basis; that is, the player does not have to spend time in a hospital. No general anesthetic is used. The stress and disruption that comes with traditional surgery is reduced dramatically.

Endoscopic surgery involves the use of an endoscope, a long thin tube equipped with a light and a camera. The surgeon makes tiny incisions in the patient's skin, inserts the tube, and sees images of the injury on a computer screen. Pencil-sized instruments, inserted through the incisions, are used to repair the damage. The most popular variation of endoscopic surgery for basketball players is arthroscopic surgery, used to repair joints. Physician Michael Brunt says, "Whether it's general surgery, hernia surgery or orthopedic

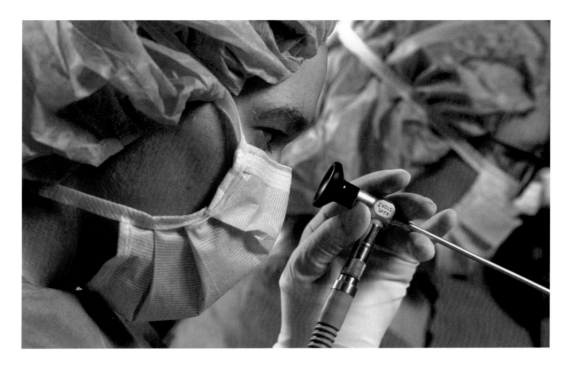

[bone, joint, ligament or muscle] surgery, things…are being done in a less invasive fashion that allows athletes to recover more quickly and get back to playing sports sooner."[29]

To repair joint damage in an athlete, doctors use an arthroscope which is inserted through a small incision.

Physical Therapy

Once players recover adequately, they start rebuilding and strengthening the part that was injured. They must also work to regain the speed and agility they once possessed. All that requires physical therapy. Physical therapy uses ultrasound, water, massage, and gentle exercise to improve the functioning of damaged muscles, bones, and joints.

Light weight-lifting is often uncomfortable therapy as players strengthen or rebuild injured muscles through the use of machines or free weights. Water therapy is more comfortable. It involves slow exercise in water, using resistance to build muscle and increase the range of joint motion.

Massage is widely used in sports medicine, but there is little scientific evidence that it is beneficial. It has not been found to change muscle strength in any way, although it does relieve soreness and stiffness. Among massage supporters, however, deep tissue massage is considered one of the best therapies to relieve severe tension in chronically damaged muscles and connective tissue. Deep tissue massage focuses on muscles deep within the body.

Career-Ending Injuries

Serious acute injuries can end a player's career, but chronic injuries, even if they are not severe, cause many retirements, too. The combined effect of many injuries can also leave players with scar tissue, arthritis, and chronic pain that makes an impact on their game. Players UCLA Bruin's Bill Walton, Chicago Bulls' Scottie Pippen, Detroit Pistons' Isiah Thomas, WNBA all-star Yolanda Griffin, and Seattle Storm's Adrienne Johnson are among the many who retired due to injuries.

Injuries are inevitable in basketball, but advances in equipment over the years have helped athletes avoid many bruises and broken bones they once suffered while playing. From courts to clothing, the development of new materials and processes have made the game more high tech and allow players to jump higher and move more easily than ever before.

CHAPTER 4

High-Tech Equipment

Just as there was no scientific training for early basketball players, there was little scientific research used in creating early uniforms and equipment for the game. Balls had irregular seams, were under- or overinflated, and were used until their covers were ragged. Shoes were leather or canvas with simple rubber soles. Clothing was lumpy, made of wool or cotton, and could be uncomfortable.

As time passed, research and new synthetic materials produced products that were more durable, comfortable, and practical. Today experts continue to study everything from shoes to scoreboards to see what can be improved.

The Surface and Below

Basketball courts have evolved from simple surfaces to high-tech systems over the years. Early courts were a simple layer of wooden planks because wood was plentiful and durable. As time passed, maple became the wood of choice. Maple is harder than other woods and thus resists scratching and other damage, yet its combination of wood fibers and air pockets make it slightly springy. This springiness absorbs some of the shock players feel when their feet hit the floor.

Beneath the synthetic or wood layer of a basketball court is a subfloor system that provides additional cushioning for players.

Recently, synthetic flooring made of interlocking tiles has become a popular alternative to hardwood. Synthetic flooring is designed to be more shock absorbing and thus easier on players' joints than hardwood. Early research, however, suggests that more injuries occur on synthetic floors than on hardwood floors.

Whether wood or synthetic, today's courts are more than just a single layer of flooring. A complex subfloor system lies beneath the surface material and provides additional cushioning for softer landings when players run or jump. There are many types of subfloors. Some are wood, cushioned with high-density foam. Others contain squishy rubber pads. One of the most common is a layer of small rubber discs filled with air and set about twelve inches (30.5cm) apart. "Think of a fancy athletic shoe that uses air-cushioned soles, and you have the right idea."[30]

Green Sports Flooring

Sports flooring manufacturers are beginning to take the environment into account when they make their products. Author Charles W. Bryant explains in the following article.

"Green is the color we just can't get enough of these days. Some companies, like EcoSport have begun to manufacture environmentally sound sports flooring. Rubber trees are used to produce latex [for rubber], but can only do so for about 25 years. When these trees are put out to pasture, EcoSport recycles them for useable hardwood. The wood is not quite as hard as maple, but is still resilient enough for use as sports flooring.

Charles W. Bryant, "What Makes Sports Flooring Different," *How Stuff Works*, 1998–2009. http://home.howstuffworks.com/home-improvement/flooring/what-makes-sports-flooring-different3.htm.

Court Standards

Basketball players know that, despite their fairly uniform appearance, courts have their own peculiarities. Some have uneven spots. Some have gouges or other damage. Some have "dead spots" where balls do not bounce as well. In an effort to standardize modern courts, beginning in 1991 manufacturers began conforming to certain performance standards. The most widely accepted were developed by the Deutsches Institut fur Normung (German Institute of Standardization) in Germany. They are known as DIN standards for hardwood floors.

Using DIN standards, manufacturers now take into account courts' shock absorption quality, their rebound potential, and their surface friction. Shock absorption is the amount of impact force a floor can absorb. Rebound potential is how well the surface allows a ball to bounce. Surface friction is the force that resists motion when the surface of one object comes into contact with the surface of another. The court should be rough enough to prevent players from slipping but smooth enough to allow them to slide their feet during play. Courts are also created with an eye for deformation control, their stability under the weight of two or more players. For instance, DIN's minimum deformation value is 2.3 millimeters (.09 inches). In other words, a court must flex at least 2.3 millimeters under the weight of two or more players. A floor with 2.2 millimeters deformation would not pass DIN. The difference in give is less than the thickness of a sheet of paper.

Performance standards do not matter if the court surface is not kept clean and dry. Anything can become an unexpected hazard. For instance, in April 2008 several players slipped on large vinyl NCAA logos that had been applied before early tournament rounds at the Raleigh, North Carolina's RBC Center. NCAA spokesman Greg Shaheen stated, "The building treated it [the logo] with a water and ammonia mix ... and the decal seemed to 'rough up' or take on a more tactile feel. At the same time, the reality is it is a contrasting surface and we need to be mindful of that."[31] They decided that they would paint the logos on in the future.

The Bouncing Ball

Basketballs have changed as much as courts and remain a focal point of the game. The first basketball was manufactured by Spalding sporting goods company in 1894. It was 32 inches (81 cm) around, made of laced leather, and weighed less than 20 ounces (567 g). Inside was a rubber bladder that was inflated to keep the ball stiff and springy.

Laces remained a part of Spalding basketballs until 1937. Leather was the material of choice for covers until 1911, when the Rawlings Sporting Goods Company made a leather and rubber composite cover. Today nearly all basketballs are made of an inflatable inner rubber bladder wrapped in layers of fiber and then covered with either leather, rubber, or a microfiber composite that absorbs sweat and is less slippery. After completion, balls are inspected for appearance, size, inflation, and wobble (uneven or unstable movement).

Some manufacturers go one step further than inspection. They subject their products to quality control tests

for designs, materials, and glues. Rawlings puts the basketballs they produce for the NCAA Tournament through a "slam machine" that imitates the workout the ball will get in a game. The machine launches a ball down a chute toward a backboard at about 30 miles per hour (48 kph). The backboard is angled to direct the ball back to the chute. Only balls that pass the workout are marketed to be used in games.

Many of today's basketballs have an inflatable rubber bladder which is wrapped in layers of fiber and is then covered with leather, rubber, or a microfiber.

The Air Inside

In addition to materials, inflation is important for basketballs because variations affect the way the ball bounces. A 22-ounce (.62 kg) ball that is correctly inflated will bounce higher with less effort than a 22-ounce ball that is underinflated. This is because air inside the ball is made up of gas particles (molecules) that have weight and volume and are in constant motion. The more molecules of air that are inside the ball, the more crowded they are and the more they move and push on the inner surface. This creates pressure and firmness. A ball with too little air is soft and hard to bounce. With too much pressure, it rebounds too high and is less controllable.

The recommended inflation pressure for basketballs is from seven to nine pounds per square inch (PSI). The organizations that use the balls dictate the precise pressure. NBA balls must be inflated to between 7.5 and 8.5 PSI. The WNBA has similar requirements. The NCAA does not use PSI inflation specification, but instead uses a bounce measurement for the balls used in their games. Men's basketballs must bounce between 49 and 54 inches (124.4 and 137.2 cm) when dropped from a height of six feet (1.8 m); for women's, the number is between 51 and 56 inches (129.5 and 142.2 cm).

Even when balls are inflated correctly, however, they slowly leak air and thus have to be checked and reinflated several times a year. In 2005 Spalding addressed that problem with the release of the Neverflat basketball, constructed of a cover with smaller pores and filled with Nitroflate molecules. Nitroflate molecules are larger than regular air molecules, so they do not seep out of the ball as quickly. A Spalding representative stated, "Groundbreaking technology developed by former NASA and Dupont scientists is at the center of the new Neverflat, the first-ever basketball guaranteed to hold air up to 10 times longer than traditional basketballs."[32]

Comfort and Practicality

Of all basketball equipment, uniforms have changed most visibly over the years. Early uniforms were quite different from the bright, comfortable sports gear worn today. Then, men wore long dark pants or baggy trousers that came just below the knee. Women wore long skirts and long-sleeved, high neck blouses. Sometimes they wore colorful scarves in team colors around their necks.

As years passed uniforms became more practical. Men adopted sleeveless wool jerseys and cotton shorts, which allowed their bodies to move easily, and rubber-soled shoes, which gripped the court. Women gave up their skirts,

which were a trip hazard, and put on knee-length bloomers. Beginning in 1936 with the All-American Redheads, a few daring women's teams began dressing in shorts and short-sleeved shirts, which were cool and allowed greater freedom of movement.

Today every article of clothing used in team play is designed for comfort and practicality. Fabrics are made of synthetic materials, such as polyester or microfiber knits or meshes, which are stretchy and comfortable. Microfiber material is also known for its softness, durability, and moisture-wicking abilities. Moisture-wicking fabrics are made with tiny holes in the weave that pull sweat away from the skin to keep players dry. It also allows for air circulation. The recent development of antimicrobial-treated fabric hinders the growth of bacteria to keep uniforms and players fresher smelling.

In early women's basketball, uniforms changed from skirts to knee-length bloomers and they wore short-sleeved shirts.

Silver Strands

Fabrics that fight bacteria that cause body odor show promise for basketball uniform manufacturers. As the following article explains, the ancient but precious metal, silver, is popular again as an antibacterial element.

"Clothing makers have discovered that adding silver ions to molten polyester is the most effective way to create antimicrobial clothing. Until now, many makers of active wear treated fabric after it was woven. Using elemental silver as an antibacterial agent is nothing new. The Egyptians used it medicinally thousands of years ago. Early American settlers put silver dollars in milk to prevent spoilage. Silver ions used in fabrics will bind to the bacteria found in perspiration. This alters the microorganisms' metabolic process to keep them from growing and giving off that familiar odor—Locker Room No. 5.

Cliff Gromer, "New High-Tech Outdoors Wearable Fabrics." *Popular Mechanics*, April 2004, p. 78.

"Looking for an Edge"

Under the uniform, many players wear specially designed underwear known as compression shorts and shirts. Women wear sports bras. All of these garments made of two-way stretch fabric sewn into a four-way stretch layer, provide support and keep muscles warm, which can help prevent injuries. Compression garments are also moisture wicking, so they help prevent chafing and rashes that damp clothing can cause.

Although players aim for safety and comfort, only a few wear mouthguards during games. Nevertheless many experts recommend these appliances to protect the teeth and mouth. Modern

SLAM DUNK

High school basketball players who wear mouthguards have ten times fewer dental injuries than those who do not.

day mouthguards are created by computers out of high-tech plastics to ensure that they fit a player's mouth exactly.

Some players like Shaquille O'Neal and Milwaukee Bucks' Michael Redd wear neuromuscular mouthguards designed to align and relax the jaw and neck while also offering shock absorption for the jaw. Better head position allows players to increase air intake and improve performance. Although the benefits of such mouthguards are debated, they are growing in popularity. "Everybody's looking for an edge over their opponent," observes pro football player Derrick Dockery, who also uses the device. "If it works, why not try it?"[33]

Converse All-Stars

Beginning in 1921 basketball shoes became a noteworthy part of every basketball uniform. Before that time players wore anything that was comfortable and durable. In 1908 shoe manufacturer Marquis Converse helped the situation a little when he founded the Converse Rubber Shoe Company in Chicago, Illinois, and began making tennis shoes. Basketball players recognized the benefits of rubber soles that gripped the court, and began wearing them during play.

Then in 1917 Converse introduced the first basketball shoe. The Converse All-Star was a simple black canvas high-top with rubber non-skid soles. It was nothing like athletic

The Converse All-Star—a simple black canvas high-top with rubber soles—became the first basketball shoe in 1917.

shoes of today, but when former basketball player Charles H. "Chuck" Taylor became a spokesman for the company in 1921, his salesmanship pushed them into the public eye. A pair of Converse All-Stars, nicknamed Chucks by their fans, became a must-have item for basketball players as well as teens across the country. Julius Erving, Magic Johnson, and Larry Bird were among the many professionals who endorsed the brand and wore them on the court throughout the years.

After Chucks the appeal of name brand athletic shoes ranging from Air Jordans to Zoom Kobes has continued nonstop. Basketball players are most concerned, however, with the shoes' construction and performance on the court. The game puts great stress and strain on their feet, so they need something that is supportive, flexible, shock absorbing, and provides proper traction or grip. To achieve that, manufacturers focus on four parts of the shoe—the uppers, insoles, midsoles, and outsoles.

Padded, Vented, and Lined

The uppers of basketball shoes are the fabric/leather portion above the sole. They provide support around the foot and ankle to prevent ankle rollover and pressure on the Achilles tendon, but are soft enough to allow flexibility. They are padded, vented, and lined with moisture-wicking fabric so the foot can remain as cool and dry as possible.

Insoles are the portion under the sole of the foot. They are firm to support players' arches. Many players replace insoles with custom-made orthotics, which are designed to relieve pressure on certain areas of the foot or to correct positioning of the lower body. Improper positioning can stem from such irregularities as overpronation (rolling in of the foot) or leg length discrepancy (one leg being shorter than the other). Without proper alignment, players can suffer ankle, knee, hip, and/or lower back pain.

Sandwiched between the insole and the bottom of the shoe (called the

SLAM DUNK

23

U.S. shoe size worn by Shaquille O'Neal.

THE ANATOMY OF A SHOE

All athletic shoes consist of four parts – an upper, an insole, a midsole, and an outsole. Basketball shoes also come in high-top, mid-top, and low-top varieties, named for the height of the upper in relation to the player's ankle. High-top shoes offer the most support for players, because the height of the upper helps with ankle stability.

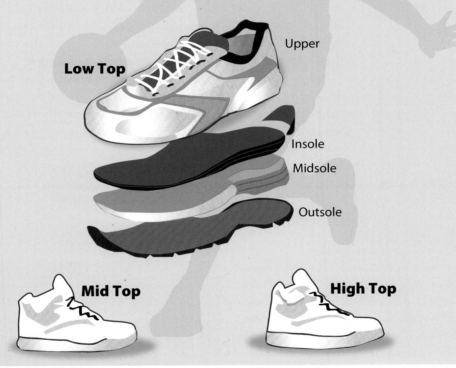

Low Top

Upper

Insole

Midsole

Outsole

Mid Top

High Top

Data: Diagram from http://www.runnersworld.com/article/0,7120,s6-240-319--10780-0,00.html, additional caption information from http://blogs.zappos.com/blogs/comfort/2008/06/15/how-shoes-are-madebasketball

"outsole"), is the midsole, which has been the focus of shoe research for more than a quarter of a century. The midsole provides cushioning and protection for the foot, and absorbs shocks to protect the knees and ankles. It must be light enough so the shoe is not too heavy, slightly spongy to absorb the force of impact with the court, and extremely durable. A balance of material is therefore necessary, and manufacturers are constantly creating new materials and shock-absorbing systems to improve performance.

Soles and Science

Most basketball midsoles are made of a combination of polyurethane and ethylene-vinyl acetate (EVA) foams. Polyurethane is stiffer and heavier than EVA, but lasts longer. EVA is softer and more flexible, but becomes flattened over time as the air is squeezed out. Once EVA is compressed, it no longer provides cushioning. Therefore, in addition to foam, manufacturers add air- or gas-filled cushions or silicone gels that help maintain insoles' bounce and cushioning.

Outsoles are the part of the shoe that comes in contact with the ground. They are usually made of real or synthetic rubber, but some are lightweight blown-synthetic rubber, which provides extra cushioning. Outsoles come in a variety of patterned treads that help players' feet grip the court

Air Jordans

In 1984 a new style of athletic shoes caught the public's attention when newcomer Michael Jordan and shoe manufacturer Nike teamed up to create Air Jordan, a breakthrough in basketball shoe design. Before the Air Jordan One (AJ I), as the new shoe came to be called, basketball shoes were black or white. Jordan's new Nikes were a bold combination of black and red, and they emphasized Jordan's uniqueness on the court.

The NBA quickly decided that wearing them violated the association's clothing policies, however. The shoes were banned, and Jordan was fined $5,000 for wearing them. Ironically, the ban helped create more publicity and interest in Nike. Recognizing a

Michael Jordan and Nike developed Air Jordans in 1984. The shoes were a breakthrough in basketball shoe design.

good thing, the company decided it would pay the fines, and Jordan continued to keep the shoes in the public eye at every game.

in a forward direction, but slide easily while shuffling or pivoting sideways.

Although players are always looking for gear that gives them an edge over their opponents, they also pay attention to the physical principles that control their every move. They know that an understanding and use of those principles can improve everything from shooting to guarding an opponent. Science educator Bill Willis says, "Understanding how things happen in a basketball game, from a physics point of view, is not necessary for a good player. [But] a physical analysis of a player's movements, combined with a knowledge of the correct forces to apply at the right time, can be used to make a good player better."[34]

CHAPTER 5

The Physics Behind the Moves

From dribbling to passing, every basketball move is governed by physics. Physics is the science of matter and energy. It is the study of how the physical world behaves, including why objects act the way they do, why they move, why they change direction, and why they stop. Journalist Saul Shandly says, "Physics plays a principle role in three areas of the game: shooting the ball into the basket, bouncing the ball, and receiving a pass."[35]

An Energetic Sport

Energy is an important term in both physics and basketball. Energy is commonly associated with vigorous activity, as in "The players are running and jumping. They have lots of energy." In physics, however, energy is defined as the ability of a physical system to do work. Everything from human beings to basketballs has energy and the Law of Conservation of Energy states that energy can be transferred, but it cannot be destroyed. Science and technology educator David E. Watson says, "Energy can be stored. Energy can move from one bunch or piece of matter to another bunch or piece of matter. Energy can be transformed from one type of energy to another type of energy. [But] during all this moving and transforming the total amount of energy never changes."[36]

Newton's Laws of Motion

Seventeenth century mathematician and physicist Sir Isaac Newton was one of the foremost scientists of all time. He first published his Laws of Motion in 1687 and used them to explain and investigate the movement of many physical objects and systems. Without his contributions, the development of modern technology would have been impossible.

First Law: If an object is at rest, it will remain at rest unless an outside force acts on it. If an object is moving, it will continue to move in a straight line at the same speed until an outside force acts on it. This is also known as the Law of Inertia.

Second Law: When a force acts on an object, the object accelerates in the direction of the force. If the mass of an object stays constant, increasing force will increase acceleration. If the force on an object remains constant, increasing mass will decrease acceleration.

Third Law: For every action there is an equal and opposite reaction, or the forces of two bodies on each other are always equal and directed in opposite directions.

In basketball as in everything else, two kinds of energy are always at play—kinetic and potential. Kinetic energy is energy of motion. The more an object weighs and the faster it is moving, the more kinetic energy it has. A ball flying through the air has kinetic energy, and so does a player leaping. Kinetic energy can transform into potential energy, which is stored energy. Potential energy exists because of an object's potential for movement or for doing work. For example, a ball held in the air by a player has potential energy because when it is released it will fall.

In addition to being classed as kinetic or potential, energy is categorized as chemical, mechanical, electrical, light, and nuclear. Basketball is all about mechanical energy, the energy of moving parts. When players shoot a basket, dribble a ball, or jump into the air, they are using mechanical energy.

A leaping basketball player demonstrates kinetic energy—the energy of motion.

Shooting the Ball

Shooting the ball toward the hoop involves several kinds of energy. For instance, the ball in the player's hands has potential energy. The player transfers energy to the ball. The ball flying through the air has kinetic energy.

The push that sends the ball flying is called a "force." A force is anything that causes change in the motion or shape of an object. A push or a pull is a force. So is the source of the push or the pull, such as the wind, a magnet, or a basketball player's hand. When force is applied to push the ball, it accelerates in the direction of the force according to how much force is applied (its magnitude). This is the basis of Newton's Second Law of Motion. Sir Isaac Newton was a seventeenth-century mathematician and

SLAM DUNK

89 feet (27 m)

Record free shot made by LA Clippers Barron Davis on February 17, 2009.

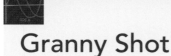

Granny Shot

No NBA player since Rick Barry in the 1970s has used the unorthodox underhand "granny shot" when shooting foul shots. Yet according to physics, the odds of scoring are much better when using Barry's method.

"The key to a successful foul shot lies in the arc of the ball—in general, the higher the better. While an official-size basket is 18 inches [45.7 cm] in diameter, the basketball itself is only about 9 1/2 inches [24.1 cm], which gives a margin of 8 1/2 inches [21.6 cm]. But when the ball is thrown nearly straight at the basket ... the margin disappears because the rim of the basket, from the perspective of the ball, resembles a tight ellipse [an oval shape]. 'That's why these guys miss so much,' [physicist Peter] Brancazio says. 'Because of the sharp angle of the typical overhand throw, there ends up being a much smaller window for the ball to go in.' If the ball comes down at the basket from a steeper angle, the way it does if tossed up in the high arc characteristic of an underhand throw, the margin reappears. 'That means there's a far greater chance of making the basket,' he says."

Curtis Rist, "Physics Proves It: Everyone Should Shoot Granny-Style," *Discover*, August 7, 2008. http://discovermagazine.com/2008/the-body/07-physics-proves-it-everyone-should-shoot-granny-style.

physicist who studied the way objects moved. His second law is also known as the Law of Acceleration, where "acceleration" is the change in speed and direction of an object over time.

Newton noted that force has both magnitude—the power of the push or pull—and direction. If the mass (amount of matter in an object) remains the same, more force results in greater acceleration and less force means less acceleration. Newton determined that the magnitude of a force can be calculated by multiplying the mass of the object being pushed or pulled by the acceleration of the object.

The Ball's Path

When the ball accelerates through the air toward the goal, it becomes a projectile. A projectile is an object which, once started by a force, continues in motion by its own inertia and

When the basketball is thrown into the air, the projectile travels in a parabolic (or U-shaped) path.

is influenced only by the downward force of gravity. Inertia is the tendency of objects to resist change in motion. Newton explained inertia in his First Law of Motion. He said that, without a force to start it, an object will never begin moving. Once it is moving, it will never stop unless acted upon by a force.

Gravity is one force that changes the motion of the ball. Gravity is the attraction that two objects have for each other, making them accelerate toward each other. The larger the masses, the bigger the pull of gravity, so on Earth, the strongest pull of gravity is toward the planet's center. This pull always causes free objects to fall or accelerate downward at 9.8 meters per second squared. So a ball thrown into the air will continue upward until its acceleration lessens and becomes less than the pull of gravity. Then the object

SLAM DUNK

18 inches (46 cm)

Diameter of standard basketball hoop.

starts to come down. The upside-down, u-shaped path that the ball takes as it goes up and then comes down is called its "parabolic path." A parabola is a curved shape that resembles a U. Another word for a parabolic path is a "trajectory."

For players to get the ball where they want it to go when they pass or shoot, they have to take into account inertia, gravity, and where the basket is in relation to where they are standing. The last factor is very important. The basket may be almost directly overhead or far across the court. A teammate may be standing tall or crouching down. Thus players must push the ball into the air at the correct angle if they want to get the ball to their teammates or through the hoop.

"A Little Bit of Physics and a Lot of Practice"

An angle is defined as the figure formed when two rays intersect. A ray is a real or imaginary line that begins at one point and extends away from that point. In practical terms, an angle looks like a slice of pie. The inner point of the slice (where the rays intersect, or meet) is called the "vertex," and its sides are the rays. Angles are measured in degrees and can range in size from zero to 360. A 360-degree angle would look like a whole pie. A 90-degree angle would look like a quarter of a pie. A zero-degree angle would look like no pie at all.

The angle at which players release a ball when shooting is called the "release angle." The vertex is at their hands, and the rays are imaginary lines, one of which runs parallel to the floor and one which follows the path of the ball when it leaves their hands. Experts have determined that players can

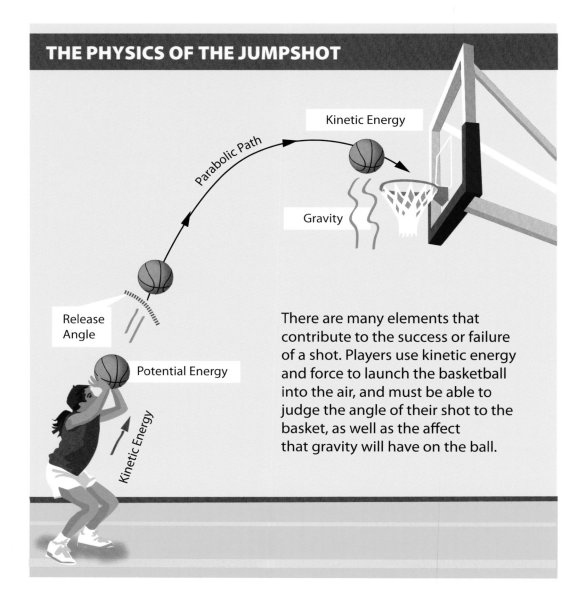

THE PHYSICS OF THE JUMPSHOT

Kinetic Energy

Parabolic Path

Gravity

Release Angle

Potential Energy

Kinetic Energy

There are many elements that contribute to the success or failure of a shot. Players use kinetic energy and force to launch the basketball into the air, and must be able to judge the angle of their shot to the basket, as well as the affect that gravity will have on the ball.

always send the ball to the center of the hoop if they create the correct release angle. That angle would depend on the height of the ball from the court, the shooter's distance from the hoop, and the force used to propel the ball. By knowing those variables, the angle can be computed. For example, a player who is 7 feet (213.3 cm) tall, shooting 15 feet (4.6 m) from the basket at a speed of 17 miles per hour (27.4 km/h) would have to shoot at an angle of 55 degrees.

Obviously the precision required to calculate and carry out such shots during the course of a game is impossible. That is why no basketball player is able to make a basket every time he shoots. However, the best shooters know that if they are consistent about when and where they release the ball, and release it with a smooth motion to get consistent speed, they will hit the basket more often. Larry Silverberg, a mechanical and aerospace engineer, studied hundreds of thousands of three-dimensional computer simulations of basketball free-throw trajectories and confirmed that fact. He says, "A little bit of physics and a lot of practice can make everyone a better shooter from the free-throw line."[37]

At the Basket

If players have the knowledge and control to use the correct force and angles when shooting a basket, the ball ends up at the hoop. If a ball drops squarely into the basket, gravity pulls it down and points are scored. If the ball hits the rim of the hoop or the backboard, other forces come into play.

When a ball hits the backboard or the rim of the basket, it encounters a force that sends it bouncing away. It does not bounce away with the same amount of force, however, because the rim or backboard absorbs a small amount of energy, and a small amount is lost due to friction. Friction is the force that resists movement between two objects. It slows or stops movement. The rougher the objects, the more friction there is between them. When the ball hits or rubs against the rim, it slows. If it hits the upper part of the rim, that slowing gives it a better chance of dropping into the basket. Fontanella writes, "Good shooters minimize the speed of the basketball at the rim. The effect of friction is to decrease the speed further. This helps any shooter."[38]

The angle at which the ball bounces away is called the rebound angle, and it is the same as the angle of entry, the angle at which the ball approached the backboard or the rim. Thus, if the ball hits the outer rim as it is coming toward the basket, it will rebound or bounce back away from the rim at that same angle. Players learn that hitting the outer front part of the rim, known as "shooting short," will never yield

If a player shoots with the correct angles and force, the basketball drops squarely into the basket while gravity pulls it down.

a goal, because the ball will always bounce away from the basket. If they hit the backboard or the back of the rim from the top, though, they have a good chance of sending the ball into the basket if its rebound angle is correct. Physics professor and basketball expert John J. Fontanella writes, "The bad news is that if a basketball hits the front of the rim at the front of the hoop, it always misses. The good news is that if a basketball hits the front of the rim at the back of the hoop, it always goes in."[39]

Backspin

A ball is more likely to bounce off a backboard and angle down through the hoop if the player gives it backspin. Backspin is rotation on a ball which slows, stops, or reverses its forward motion. With backspin the ball rotates backward at the same time it flies through the air. Because it is spinning backward when it hits the backboard, it does not hit as hard as it would if it were spinning forward. It also has more of a tendency to bounce in the direction of its spin, which is downward and backward, toward the net. "Back spin deadens the ball [reduces its upward energy] when it bounces off the rim or backboard … giving [it] a better chance of settling through the net,"[40] says journalist Mick Kulikowski.

Players produce backspin by flicking their wrists forward and down as the ball rolls off their fingers when they shoot. This downward motion of the wrists starts the ball spinning toward them. Although the ball is spinning backward, the greater force of their arms pushes it forward through the air. When backspin is correctly combined with trajectory, friction, gravity, and bounce back, the ball takes a path down through the hoop. If the combination of forces is wrong, the shot is missed.

Researcher Silverberg calculated that shooters should launch their shots with about three hertz of backspin. A hertz is a unit of frequency equal to one cycle per second. That means the ball should make three complete backspinning revolutions before reaching the hoop. Because most players do not have the time or control needed to determine the frequency of their backspin, practice and consistency is again the best rule. "Practice is the key to becoming a better shooter," says sports writer Daniella Gardino. "Practice makes perfect."[41]

Jumping Skills

While players need to be able to handle the ball well to get it into the basket, at the same time they need good jumping skills. Center jumps, slam dunks, and layups are three plays that require players to bend their knees and use their leg muscles to push off the floor with explosive force. The best jumpers get farther off the ground, because they weigh less and/or have more powerful leg muscles than other players.

An average NBA player can jump vertically 28 inches (71.1 cm), and any vertical jump over 36 inches (91.4 cm) is considered exceptional. The height of the players is not always an indication of their vertical jump, however. Retired NBA star Spudd Webb is only 5 foot 7 inches (170.1 cm), but he had a leap of 46 inches (116.8 cm). That was almost as high as 6 foot 6 inch (198.1 cm) Michael Jordan, who had a leap of 48 inches

Numerous basketball moves like slam dunks, lay ups, and center jumps require the athlete to have good jumping skills.

(121.9 cm). On the other hand, 6 foot 9 inch (205.7 cm) players Karl Malone and Magic Johnson had only 28-inch (71.1 cm) and 30-inch (76.2 cm) vertical jumps respectively.

Vertical jumps are important, but players seldom move straight upward when they jump during a game. Instead, they take a few steps and then launch themselves forward and upward in a parabolic arc similar to the path a ball follows when it is thrown. Despite the fact that their bodies travel in an arc, many appear to defy the laws of gravity and hang in the air for a time. Nobel-Prize-winning scientist Kary Mullis writes, "It seems they are not really following a physical trajectory sometimes. Now whether that's the truth or not, it feels that way, anyway. They just keep hanging up there."[42]

Hang Time

"Hang time" is that moment during which players seem to float in the air when they jump. Elgin Baylor and Michael Jordan were renowned for their hang time. In fact, hang time is an illusion (a false impression). During a jump the body moves up and forward, reaches a high point, and then comes down. The whole time in the air is actually no more than one second. Willis writes, "If you used a stopwatch and a slow-motion replay, you would discover that the time from when [the player] left the floor to when he stops moving upward is exactly equal to the time he takes to fall. ... The instant he stops going up, he starts to fall. But this is hard to see when things happen fast and there is forward movement."[43]

The illusion is created because of two circumstances. First, players move their arms upward and pull their legs up as they reach the height of their leap. This heightens the impression of upward movement. Second, they actually lengthen the time they are in the air by leaping forward as well as upward. The physics of the trajectory does the rest.

At the beginning and end of the trajectory, vertical speed is greatest, while at the top of the top of the trajectory, just before players start coming down, vertical speed nears zero. So as they near the highest part of their jump, they are not moving vertically as much as they are moving horizontally.

They are also in the air longest during this time, and they are highly visible. Coupled with techniques like lifting the arms and legs to give the appearance of upward motion, the combination works so they appear to be defying gravity and floating.

Dribbling the Ball

In addition to jumping and shooting the ball, players spend a great deal of time dribbling. In this move, energy, gravity, friction, and angles all play significant roles. The ball has potential energy when it is held in the player's hands.

As a player dribbles the basketball, potential energy turns into kinetic energy when the ball is pushed downward.

Friction and Basketball

Friction, the force that opposes motion between two objects, plays an important role in basketball. First, because it is resistance to movement, it must be constantly overcome. In order to start running, for example, players must exert energy to counteract static friction between their shoes and the floor. They have to take into account that kinetic or dynamic friction, which occurs when two surfaces rub against each other, will slow the ball as it rolls across the court.

Friction is also helpful in the game of basketball. Without friction, players would slide uncontrollably around the court when they tried to stop running. As author James Clark says in *The Physics of Basketball*, "Although friction can make the game more difficult, the game itself would be impossible to play if friction didn't exist."

James Clark, "Running and Stopping." The Physics of Basketball, 2001. http://the-physicsofbasketball.homestead.com/running.html.

Its potential energy becomes kinetic energy as soon as it is pushed downward. Gravity pulls it downward, too, so coupled with the mechanical energy from the player, the downward movement is faster than it would be if the ball were pulled by gravity alone.

The moment the ball hits the floor, kinetic energy again becomes potential, and some of it is lost through friction. Willis explains, "As the ball meets the ground, it deforms, and some of the kinetic energy gets stored in the molecules of the ball as they bend, just like in a spring. But some of the energy is lost as heat, as the molecules twist, and some more goes into warming the floor slightly [because of friction]."[44] Because of lost energy, and with the pull of gravity to overcome, when the ball bounces upward it does not rise to its original height. Each bounce that follows drains energy, so eventually it settles to the floor. For that reason, dribbling requires the player's hand to add energy in the form of a push after each bounce.

Just as when they shoot, players must take angles into account when they dribble. When a ball is thrown from a player's hand to the floor, it creates what is known as an "angle of incidence," measured between the floor and the ball's path. If the ball travels straight down, the angle of incidence is 90 degrees. Angles of incidence are always 90 degrees or less. The angle at which the ball travels away from the floor after the bounce is called the angle of reflection. The Law of Reflection says that under ideal conditions, the angle of incidence always equals the angle of reflection, so the ball always bounces up and away at the same angle that it hits the floor. Ideal conditions mean that the ball is perfectly round, the floor is hard, flat, and perfectly clean, and the ball is not spinning. Taking into account angles of incidence and reflection, players know that when they angle a ball toward the floor, it will bounce up and away at the same angle, and they will have to run ahead to that spot to intercept it.

Blocking and Receiving

When one player blocks an opponent or intercepts the ball from that opponent, another physics term—*resistance*—comes into play. Resistance is a force that hinders or opposes motion, and, when it is present, a player must overcome it, if an object is to move. Friction is resistance. The floor is resistance. Often, resistance is a player standing in front of another player, blocking his path.

Players are sources of resistance to the ball when they receive or catch it. Because of them, the ball stops. Its kinetic energy is transferred to them. Usually that energy is transferred to their hands, where the force of impact can be painful. The sting of this contact can be lessened, if they take more time to catch the ball. They can do this either by moving their hands and arms slightly back or by taking a step backward as the ball hits. In both situations they are giving the ball more time to slow down and adding to the time that energy is transferring. Experts call the ability to absorb impact "soft hands." Coach Joe Waters says, "Soft hands is a term that is used to describe a players' ability to handle the basketball regardless of how hard or soft it comes at them. They seem to be able to control everything."[45]

Whether it is soft hands or better balance, players' knowledge of their physical abilities and how their bodies work is another important part of basketball. From stance to coordination, there is plenty to learn both on the court and off.

CHAPTER 6

Bodies in Motion

B asketball players' movements on the court are often astounding to those who watch them. Film director Woody Allen, a New York Knicks fan, recalls his feelings watching All-Star Earl Monroe. "He would dart into a group of guys and spin and pivot and duck under and turn around. It looked like his hands and feet were going off in every direction at the same time. [Then] the ball would go up and he would make the shot."[46]

The coordination of nerves, muscles, and organs needed to carry out such movements is complicated. Just dribbling a ball or shooting a basket calls for everything from eyes to leg muscles to work in finely tuned harmony.

20/20

Eyes are important to any athlete. The part of the eye that takes in images is the retina, a complex layered structure on the eyeball's inner surface. The retina contains photoreceptor cells that detect light and color. Its center is responsible for sharp central vision. Its edges are responsible for peripheral or side vision. Visual images that the retina picks up trigger messages that travel through the optic nerve to the brain.

Six muscles around the outside of each eye work together to move the eyeballs up and down, and to coordinate them so they move together. These muscles help the eyes focus, so

EYE MUSCLES IN FOCUS

Left eye, see from the side (lateral rectus facing out of head, medial rectus facing towards nose):

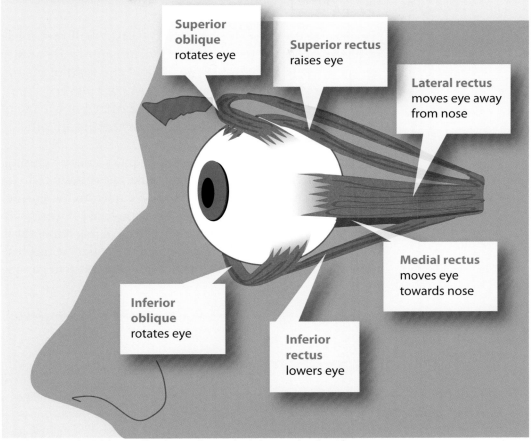

Superior oblique rotates eye

Superior rectus raises eye

Lateral rectus moves eye away from nose

Medial rectus moves eye towards nose

Inferior oblique rotates eye

Inferior rectus lowers eye

Data from http://health.howstuffworks.com/human-body/systems/eye/eye1.htm

they can see images clearly both near and far. They also help players track images—follow the ball and other teammates with their eyes.

Having two eyes that work together contributes to players' depth perception, their ability to see the court in three dimensions. When the eyes send a picture of an object from two slightly different angles, the brain is able to judge the distance to that object with a high degree of accuracy.

Without depth perception, players would have greater difficulty making baskets or completing passes because they could not easily determine how far they needed to throw the ball.

Eyes and Hands

Peripheral vision is so important in basketball that it has a special name—court vision. Court vision is the ability to see what is going on at the edge of the field of vision, including action that might be almost over players' shoulders. Players with court vision have greater knowledge of what is going on and can be ready to react more quickly than they otherwise would.

Using court vision, players can avoid someone coming up on them from the side and can make last minute changes in passing to get the ball where they want it to be. Former Utah Jazz guard John Stockton is an example of someone with excellent court vision. Sports writer Mark Welling remembers, "The vision which Stockton possessed seemed to be magical. He could find ways of fitting passes into non-existent passing

The Nervous System

The nervous system, made up of the brain, spinal cord, and a network of nerves that threads through the body and governs the movement, balance, and coordination necessary to play basketball.

"What are nerves? They're the thin threads of nerve cells called neurons that run throughout your body.

… The fingers of one neuron almost reach to the next neuron. When a neuron is stimulated—by heat, cold, touch, sound vibrations or some other message—it begins to actually generate a tiny electrical pulse. This electricity and chemical change travels the full length of the neuron. But when it gets to the end of finger-like points at the end of the neuron, it needs help getting across to the next extended finger. That's where chemicals come in. The electrical pulse in the cells triggers the release of chemicals that carry the pulse to the next cell. And so on and so on and so on."

"Nervous System," *Discovery Communications*, 2000. http://yucky.discovery.com/flash/body/pg000136.html.

lanes. Stockton was always three or four steps ahead of the defenders."[47]

Eye-hand coordination is just as important as court vision. Eye-hand coordination is the ability of the brain to direct eyes and hands to work together in order to perform tasks such as reaching and grasping. It is based on the functioning of proprioreceptors, which are specialized sensory receptors on nerve endings found in muscles, tendons, joints, and the inner ear. These receptors relay information about motion or position.

Proprioreceptors help players make baskets, dribble, and pass with great accuracy. When their eyes see the basket, their brains direct their hands to shoot so the ball goes toward it. Steve Nash of the Phoenix Suns is an example of a player with great eye-hand coordination. Basketball consultant Randy Brown writes about Nash, "He is deceptively quick, resourceful, and a great shooter, able to penetrate, a master playmaker, and a pinpoint passer."[48]

The "Balance System"

Proprioreceptors are also important in balance, the ability to remain stable despite changes in body position. Good balance is essential in playing basketball. It allows for power, control, and accuracy in shooting, dribbling, passing, and other moves. All plays are more successful with good body balance.

In addition to proprioreceptors, the eyes and ears are involved in balance. The eyes function by giving the brain visual cues about whether the body is vertical, upside down, lying flat, or in some other position. The ears, specifically the inner ears, hold a fluid-filled structure called the "labyrinth," which is responsible for sensations of motion and balance. Specialist John Epley states, "The 'balance system' is a reflex system that allows us to maintain awareness of our spatial orientation at all times, and react to it. Without it, we could not walk upright or follow objects with our eyes when we are moving."[49]

Sixth Sense

Proprioception is a little known term, but it helps control body movements. Sports therapist Todd Hargove explains in the following article.

"Proprioception is sometimes called the 6th sense—it is the brain's ability to sense the position, movement and speed of all the muscles and joints in the body. Proprioception can be thought of as the brain's 3-D map of the body. Because of proprioception, we are able to know exactly where our hand is as it moves through space, even if our eyes are closed. How is this possible? There are millions of microscopic organs called mechanoreceptors located throughout the body. When they are stimulated by a mechanical force, they send a signal to a part of the brain devoted to sensing that part of the body. The brain assembles all these signals from the innumerable different sources and determines exactly where everything is and what it is doing. In essence, the brain creates a virtual map of the body that it uses to decide how to move."

Todd Hargrove, "Proprioception: The 3-D Map of the Body," *Better Movement*, September 12, 2008. http://toddhargrove.wordpress.com/2008/09/12/proprioception-the-3-d-map-of-the-body/.

Triple-Threat Position

A good stance (physical position) while playing the game goes far toward helping maintain good balance. The triple-threat stance is standard in basketball because it allows players to be physically steady and ready to pass, dribble, or shoot instantaneously. Author Jon Oliver says, "For Michael Jordan, effective use of the triple-threat position often resulted in his strongly taking the basketball to the basket and dunking with authority."[50]

In the triple-threat position, players crouch slightly so their center of gravity is closer to the floor. Center of gravity is the center of mass of an object, the point around which

The triple-threat position (shown by the defensive player in the picture) allows a player to be ready to shoot, dribble, or pass instantly.

all weight is evenly distributed. Depending on how human beings position themselves, their center of gravity changes, with the center shifting to where the weight is most concentrated. When players are standing, their centers of gravity are somewhere just above their waists. The closer their center of gravity is to the floor, the lower their weight is to the floor, the less likely they are to overbalance, and the more stable they are.

In addition to a lower center of gravity, a larger base of support also increases stability. In the triple-threat stance, players increase their base of support by placing their feet flat on the floor, about shoulder width apart, with one foot slightly ahead of the other. The head is slightly forward, the back is straight. Knees and elbows are bent and relaxed. In this position, potential energy is also stored, ready to be used when legs and arms are straightened.

Controlled Movement

Motor coordination, the organized working together of muscles to bring about purposeful movement such as walking or jumping, is a physical necessity for basketball. Coordination is controlled by the part of the brain called the "cerebellum," located in the back of the head. Players use coordination when they move their bodies, arms, legs, and heads smoothly and without wasted energy on the court.

Balanced muscle reaction is an element of good motor coordination. This is when muscle groups contract and relax the correct amount at the proper time. Dribbling, for instance, involves the appropriate mix of contractions and extensions of muscle groups in the arm. When muscle reaction is balanced, players are able to dribble accurately and easily. Without balanced reactions they are likely to fumble the ball, or lose control of it.

Rhythm or timing is another element of coordination. Timing is the ability to make body movements dovetail with outside factors. Catching a ball involves timing so that the ball (an outside factor) and the hands meet at the right time. Timing is a combination of decision-making, balanced muscle reaction, and appropriate reaction time, and involves the brain, nerves, eyes, and muscles all working together. Good timing helps players regulate or pace their movements. It also helps them be at the right place at the right time to carry out the extremely complex moves of basketball. For instance, in the two-person

SLAM DUNK

75 to 120

Number of times the average basketball player jumps during a game.

alley-oop move, one player must get the ball, spin, and throw it to a teammate who must be in the right place to be able to jump, catch the ball in midair, spin, and shoot the ball into the basket. Timing helps both players to think in tandem in addition to moving smoothly and without wasted effort.

Reflexes, Reaction Time, and the Competitive Edge

Coordination is vital for basketball, but without quick reflexes players would not be able to make the lightning-like pivots, throws, and catches that are common in basketball. Reflexes are automatic responses to stimuli, and players must not only have great innate reflexes, they must have excellent conditioned ones as well. An innate reflex, such as blinking one's eyes, is inborn. A conditioned reflex, such as blocking an

Blocking an opponent's shot is a conditioned reflex.

opponent or jumping for a rebound, is learned. It becomes automatic only after much practice.

Players with quick reflexes have very short reaction times. Reaction time is the time it takes to respond after receiving a stimulus. It is generally fastest when only one logical response can be made. For example, when a person touches a hot stove, the first response is to pull away, and the move takes place in a fraction of a second.

When there is more than one possible response, however, reaction times may be longer. For instance, if a player has to decide whether to shoot or pass the ball, he has to think, even if only for a split second. Reaction time can be reduced, if players know what to expect and are prepared to react. In basketball, knowing what to expect means understanding every aspect of the game extremely well. It also means studying opponents' moves and mannerisms. Sport and fitness training consultant Denise K. Wood notes, "Delays in responses can make the difference between winning and losing. Athletes who can accelerate the decision-making process have a competitive edge over their opponents."[51]

Ball Handling

Ball-handling skills are the techniques players use when they touch and/or control the ball during the game. Good ball handling involves good eye-hand coordination, quick reflexes, and patience to practice until they master each technique. Players with the best skills are usually those who learn them early in life, so that they come naturally. NBA All-Star "Pistol" Pete Maravich was an example of such a pro. Maravich, who was given his first basketball at the age of seven, fell asleep in bed at night while practicing the backspin, follow through, and release techniques learned from his father. He continued to practice ball handling almost nonstop throughout his childhood. Eventually he could dribble a ball while riding his bicycle, dribble blindfolded, and spin a ball on his fingertips without looking.

Maravich knew what all players know—that good ball handling requires the use of correct techniques. For better control they touch the ball with spread fingers and not the palm. Dribbling is carried out by firmly pushing the ball downward using fingers and finger pads (the fleshy underside of the fingers). Passing involves placing the hands on either side of the ball. Arms are then extended to push the ball away from the chest, using the wrists to give it extra force. In receiving, fingers lock firmly onto the ball as soon as it touches the hands.

Handling the ball correctly while shooting is vital to consistently score points. To begin, the ball is not gripped, but rests lightly on the fingers and finger pads of the shooting hand. The fingers are spread wide to provide a stable base on which the ball rests. The other hand merely supports the ball. Elbows are bent and close to the body. When the shooting arm straightens, it raises and launches the ball, which must roll off the fingers. The shooting hand then follows through with a snap of the wrist downward. Shooting coach Buzz

Your Personal Vertical Leap

A vertical leap is the height a person can jump straight up off the ground from a standing position. To measure your vertical leap, stand with your side against the wall and extend your arm upward as high as it can reach. Make a mark there with a pencil or piece of chalk. That mark is known as your vertical reach.

Next, in the same position and with your arm still stretched upward, jump vertically as high as possible. Make a second mark on the wall at that height. Measure the distance between the two marks. The difference is your vertical leap.

A vertical leap is performed by jumping straight off the ground from a standing position.

Braman says, "To be a complete offensive player, a consistent ... shot is a must. Hot-and-cold shooting is a product of mechanical flaws in the stroke."[52]

Hot and cold shooting—sometimes making every shot and at other times being unable to score—can also be the result of a poor mental outlook. When players adopt beliefs and attitudes that shake their confidence or undermine their self-worth, it can seriously affect their performance. Being mentally ready to play a winning game of basketball is just as important as knowing the physics and physiology of the sport. As psychologist and former NCAA consultant Alan Goldberg says, "Your basketball skills and moves on the court are only as good as your head. Your physical game is always limited by your mental one."[53]

CHAPTER 7

The Psychology of Winning

P sychology, the science of the mind and behavior, is an important part of the game of basketball. The desire to compete is entirely psychological, and it is what drives athletes to want to win. Other thought processes determine their likelihood of success or failure, too. Those processes include concentrating or maintaining focus, having confidence or a belief in one's own abilities, and having emotional control. Coach and author Hal Wissel says, "Basketball is a mental, as well as a physical, game. Developing the mental aspect is a key to enhancing shooting as well as performance in all fundamentals."[54]

Competition and Stress

From the moment Naismith invented basketball in 1896, players competed with each other to win. Competition is a psychological process that involves trying to do one's best and/or trying to do better than others. In sports it means that two or more parties are going for a goal, a win, or a prize that cannot be shared. The rewards for winning may simply be a sense of pride. In professional basketball monetary awards also go to the winners.

THE BRAIN'S STRESS RESPONSE

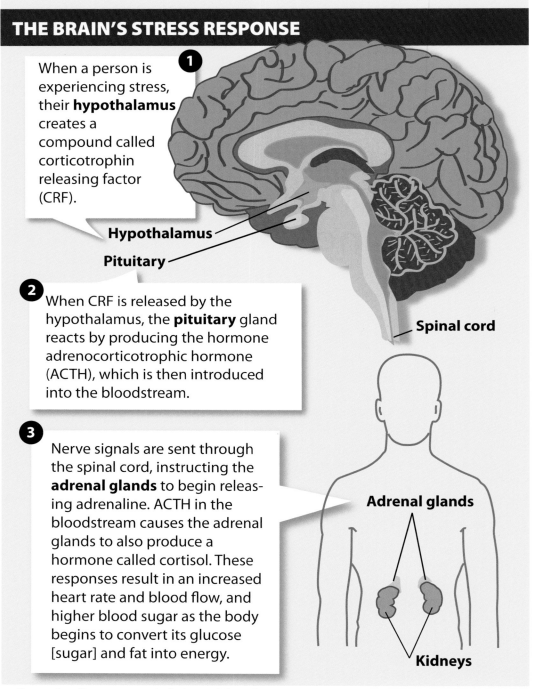

1 When a person is experiencing stress, their **hypothalamus** creates a compound called corticotrophin releasing factor (CRF).

Hypothalamus

Pituitary

2 When CRF is released by the hypothalamus, the **pituitary** gland reacts by producing the hormone adrenocorticotrophic hormone (ACTH), which is then introduced into the bloodstream.

Spinal cord

3 Nerve signals are sent through the spinal cord, instructing the **adrenal glands** to begin releasing adrenaline. ACTH in the bloodstream causes the adrenal glands to also produce a hormone called cortisol. These responses result in an increased heart rate and blood flow, and higher blood sugar as the body begins to convert its glucose [sugar] and fat into energy.

Adrenal glands

Kidneys

Sources: http://www.youramazingbrain.org.uk/brainchanges/stressbrain.htm,
http://www.medicinenet.com/stress/page5.htm, http://stress.about.com/od/stresshealth/a/cortisol.htm

Seven Secrets of Success

Team Spirit can boost the chances of success for any basketball team. Author and motivator Paul Davis gives seven secrets to building team spirit and a winning attitude in sports.

1. Uphold and honor the team effort above individual performance, while remembering a solid collective performance from individual players contributes to the quality of the team.
2. Harness your tongue and avoid complaining, remembering that noisy negatives distract from the team focus and goals.
3. Lay your ego down so the team can succeed and abound.
4. Honor and acknowledge every team member's vital contribution.
5. Encourage and empower every teammate to succeed.
6. Practice as passionately as you expect to play on game day.
7. Attend to the devil in the details. Defeat happens because of little mistakes that prove costly.

Paul Davis, "Cultivating Team Spirit and a Winning Attitude to Achieve Peak Performance and Win Games as a Team," *Ezine Articles.com*, 2009. http://ezinearticles.com/?Cultivating-Team-Spirit-and-a-Winning-Attitude-to-Achieve-Peak-Performance-and-Win-Games-As-a-Team&id=1244315.

Competition makes basketball more exciting for players and fans. But it also creates stress. Stress is physical, mental, or emotional strain or tension that occurs in response to pain, high demand situations, and/or uncertainty. Stress causes a body to produce the hormones adrenaline and cortisol. Together they make the heart beat faster, blood pressure rise, muscles tighten, and senses sharpen. These physical changes can increase players' strength and stamina, speed their reaction time, and enhance their focus. All are qualities needed to play a better game.

Stress can also be negative and overwhelming to players, though. For instance, if a family member is sick and a big game is coming up, a player might find it difficult to cope with both at the same time. Overwhelming stress can lead to physical symptoms such as headaches, digestive upsets, and sleep disorders. It can also express itself through depression, irritability, inability to concentrate, and lack of confidence.

Competitive Anxiety

When stress begins to seriously affect performance on the court, players are said to be exhibiting performance or competitive anxiety. That anxiety can be measured by tests such as the Sports Competition Anxiety Test (SCAT), developed by sports experts Rainier Martens, Robin S. Vealey, and Damon Burton in the 1990s. Levels of anxiety are determined by athletes' responses to a series of statements about how they feel in a competitive situation. Statements might include, "Before I compete I feel uneasy" and "When I compete I worry about making mistakes." Behavior on the court also gives clues to players' mindsets. They may be unfocused and nervous. They may fumble the ball. They may "choke" or fail at the moment they need to do well. In contrast, players who do well when asked to perform under pressure are called "clutch" players.

Performance anxiety can lead to a downward spiral of more bad performance. The worse players do on the court, the more anxious and tense they become. They replay mistakes in their heads until they can think of little else. Sports psychologist Saul Miller says, "If somebody is not playing well, they tend to think again and again about negative stuff. It's like a squirrel running around on an activity wheel in their minds."[55]

Players use relaxation, positive thinking, and trigger words to avoid or relieve anxiety. With relaxation they take deep breaths and relax their muscles. They put aside stressful thoughts for a time. Positive thinking is a practice that retrains the mind to be more hopeful and optimistic through the repetition of positive mental statements. With positive thinking athletes replace critical self-talk with positive pep talks. For example, they say, "I know I can do it," rather than "Don't miss this crucial free throw." Trigger words are words that start a way of thinking or a course of action. With positive trigger words, players remind themselves to perform the correct moves. Some repeat the word "Point!" just before they release the ball off the index finger. Or they say "High!" if they want to keep the ball high as they shoot.

Concentration, Confidence, and Control

Stress and anxiety are more likely to be kept under control if players have good concentration—the ability to focus completely on the job at hand. Concentration helps block out other

Michael Jordan is said to have exhibited amazing mental concentration when he was in the NBA.

distractions. It allows players to pay attention to the play they are supposed to carry out even in the midst of noise and confusion on and around the court. It helps them temporarily ignore personal problems, anger, worry, and even pain. Chicago Bulls' Stacey King recalls of Michael Jordan, "MJ's special strength was his ability to play through pain. He just blocked out the pain of a sprained ankle or foot injury and wouldn't miss a game. Most guys would be out for two weeks, but not MJ. His focus and mental toughness were awesome."[56]

The Pause

Angry outbursts by players on the basketball court illustrate the need for emotional control in sports. A valuable part of control involves the ability to pause. Despite excitement or stress, everyone is able to stop and think before giving way to his or her feelings.

Pausing only takes a moment. It must be long enough, however, to let the consequences of an emotional outburst run through the mind. Players could remember that swearing at the coach will result in an expensive fine. Or they could recall that attacking an opponent might mean expulsion from the game or worse. NBA star Dennis Rodman's uncontrolled behavior on at least two occasions—when he head-butted a referee on March 16, 1996, and when he kicked a cameraman in the groin on January 15, 1997—cost him hundred of thousands of dollars in fines and eventually led to his leaving the NBA. As many great players can testify, learning to pause is difficult to master at first, but with will power and determination, it is worth the effort.

Dennis Rodman's lack of behavioral control eventually led to his leaving the NBA.

Confidence is another quality that carries players through stressful times. Instead of allowing themselves to respond with anxiety or discouragement, they choose to believe in themselves. They reject the thought that they have to be perfect and instead adopt mottos such as "My mistakes don't define me," and "Don't worry about losing. Think about winning." They continue to believe they have talent, and they keep trying to correct mistakes. Psychologist Jim Taylor notes, "A deep faith in your capabilities comes from total preparation, exposure to adversity, support from others, and training and competitive success."[57]

Emotional control is vital if players are going to maintain concentration on the court. They must be able to put aside worries, fears, and other distractions so that they can focus on the job at hand. Anger is one emotion that, when uncontrolled, can have disastrous consequences for players and even entire teams. When the Detroit Pistons and Indiana Pacers were playing at the Palace of Auburn Hills outside Detroit, Michigan, on November 19, 2004, Piston center Ben Wallace was fouled by Pacer Ron Artest. Wallace then shoved Artest, other teammates got involved, and within minutes a huge fight broke out involving players, fans, and coaches. Nine players were eventually suspended without pay for a total of 146 games, leading to a loss of $10 million in salary. Five were also charged with assault and were sentenced to a year on probation and community service.

"Until Russell Throws Up"

Many players rely on superstitious to give themselves a feel of greater control before and during games. Superstitions are based on a belief that certain events or outcomes can be influenced by unrelated actions. Many players believe that by performing rituals linked to such beliefs, they can be more successful. And despite the fact that superstitions are not based on reason, one 2010 study at the University of Cologne in Germany revealed that they improve performance by giving participants a feeling of confidence. Because of that, participants set their goals higher, too. "Our results suggest that the activation of a superstition

SLAM DUNK

Michael Jordan, a graduate of North Carolina, always wore his blue North Carolina shorts under his Bulls uniform for good luck.

can indeed yield performance-improving effects,"[58] says Lysann Damisch, co-author of the study.

The list of superstitions in basketball is long and varied. NBA Hall of Fame member Karl Malone believed that wearing the same pair of socks during every game of the season helped him play better. Retired Los Angeles Lakers guard Jerry West drove the same complicated route to the Los Angeles Forum before every one of his home games. Dallas Mavericks owner Mark Cuban, who does not hold with superstitions, observes, "Every locker room has a comical procession of superstitions. We have things based on time, on speech intonations and on specific conversation exchanges."[59]

Even coaches have their superstitions. Boston Celtics coach Red Auerbach did not allow the team on the court until Bill Russell, who had a nervous stomach, threw up. Celtics guard John Havlicek remembers, "Red said, 'I don't care if there's 15,000 people out there, a national television audience and everyone else waiting, we're not going … on the court until Russell throws up.'"[60]

Commander or Guide

Coaches like Red Auerbach strongly influence the mental outlook of basketball players. Coaches encourage; they give advice; they solve problems; they provide the overall winning plan. Los Angeles Lakers' coach Phil Jackson says, "I think the most important thing about coaching is that you have to have a sense of confidence about what you're doing. You have to be a salesman and you have to get your players, particularly your leaders, to believe in what you're trying to accomplish on the basketball floor."[61]

Coaches use different approaches to motivate players. Some command, criticize, and demand. They give players no voice, but instead insist that the athletes only listen and obey. Former NCAA coach Bobby Knight is an example of such a commander-coach. Knight was well-known for shouting insults and obscenities at the Indiana Hoosiers for twenty-nine years. Nevertheless he led the team to years of championships. He also helped the U.S. national basketball team earn gold at the summer Olympics in 1984. Alan Henderson, who played under Knight, recalls, "He got on me sometimes like he got on everybody but he knew I could take that and I never let it get me down and I just kept pushing through it."[62]

Player-turned-coach Larry Bird had a different style. He was a positive motivator who preferred a cooperative teaching style. So does Jackson. Both men shared decision-making with

A Coach's Wisdom

Renowned coach Arnold Jacob "Red" Auerbach was a pioneer of modern basketball, redefining the game so it was dominated by team play and tough defensive work instead of individual triumphs and high scoring. An early example of the positive-motivator coach, Auerbach continually impressed on his players the importance of solid fundamental skills and unselfish team cooperation. Despite his hatred of losing, he always treated his players with respect. He stated, "Players are people, not horses. You don't handle them. You work with them, you coach them, you teach them, and, maybe most important, you listen to them."

Quoted in Matt Schudel, "Red Auerbach Dies at 89," *Washington Post*, October 29, 2006. www.washingtonpost.com/wp-dyn/content/article/2006/10/28/AR2006102801102_2.html.

Coach "Red" Auerbach impressed the importance of teamwork on his players.

the players while providing guidance when necessary. Both demanded excellence, but encouraged cooperation and team spirit. The success of their approach was apparent as their teams won championship after championship. Jackson, for instance, is the first and only coach to win ten championships in any of North America's major sports. "It's his ability to bring people together," says Kobe Bryant. "That's the biggest thing that he does so well—he continues to coach the group, continues to coach unity and chemistry and togetherness. Because when you're together, you can withstand adversity."[63]

Team Chemistry

The ability of a coach and his team to work together and get along well is called "team chemistry." Team chemistry has to do with emotions. It is interaction between people who cooperate, respect each other, and share good memories. Team chemistry takes place when each player is willing to work hard, play unselfishly, communicate well, and take responsibility for his or her own and each others' actions. Former New York mayor Mario Cuomo observes, "The [New York] Knicks players … understood the need for community. They all played that way, which is a testament to their coach, Red Holzman, as well as to the individuals themselves. They won by understanding that five people who are well synchronized, who are selfless … will make it better for the community overall."[64]

Sometimes it takes only one player to spark team chemistry. Former NBA greats Magic Johnson and Bill Bradley were known for their generous assistance to other teammates and for their team play on the court. Former Portland Trailblazer Bill Walton inspired a sense of team spirit by constantly warning his teammates of opponents' plays and encouraging them with the phrase "Hey, we love ya!" His coach, John Wooden recalls, "There have been many great players in the game, but not many great team players. Walton is a very great team player."[65]

Even the best players discover that there are benefits of team chemistry. Michael Jordan initially relied only on himself when he played. He scored dozens of points, but his team did not always win. Coach Jackson says, "I tried to make him understand that to win a championship, he had to share the ball. He had to share the limelight. He had to share some of the glory."[66] When Jordan learned how to delegate and work with his teammates, they were together able to win three championships in a row.

Great teams do not always have team chemistry, and good chemistry cannot make a bad team into champions. But if players like each other and are united in going for the same goals, they are more likely to have greater success than expected.

Despite that, many players and fans see team chemistry as relatively unimportant. They are convinced that what counts is whether players have strong muscles, quick reflexes, and star quality. James Naismith, however, would disagree. He believed that the way the game was played was more important than winning. "Be strong in body, clean in mind, lofty in ideals,"[67] he urged. Of the three parts of his statement, two focus on beliefs and character. The science behind sport is fascinating, but it is spirit of the players that gives the game heart and makes it extraordinary.

NOTES

Chapter 1: Peach Baskets and Playoffs

1. Quoted in Michael Levenson and Andrew Ryan, "Hoop Heaven." *The Boston Globe*, June 20, 2008. www.boston.com/sports/basketball/celtics/articles/2008/06/20/hoop_heaven/?page=2.

2. Quoted in Allison Cumbow, "Paying Tribute to James Naismith, the Man Who Started It All." *The University Daily Kansan*, February 15, 2008. www.kansan.com/news/2008/feb/15/paying_tribute_james_naismith_man_who_started_it_a/.

3. Quoted in Robert W. Peterson, *Cages to Jumpshots*. New York: Oxford University Press, 1990, p. 21.

4. Quoted in Peterson, *Cages to Jumpshots*, p. 20.

5. Senda Berenson Abbot. "Basket Ball at Smith College." *Spalding's Athletic Library*, c. 1914, pp. 69–77. http://clio.fivecolleges.edu/smith/berenson/5pubs/bball_smith/index.shtml?page=4.

6. Quoted in Peterson, *Cages to Jumpshots*, pp. 46–47.

7. Quoted in Peterson, *Cages to Jumpshots*, p. 130.

8. Sally Jenkins. "History of Women's Basketball." *WNBA*, 2009. www.wnba.com/about_us/jenkins_feature.html.

Chapter 2: The Discipline of Training

9. Steven M. Traina. "NBA Players Always in Training." *ESPN*, 2007. http://espn.go.com/trainingroom/s/fitness/index.html.

10. Traina, "NBA Players Always in Training."

11. Quoted in Jerry Tarkanian, "Basketball Shooting Is Both Art and Science." *Coach Like a Pro*, 2009. www.coachlikeapro.com/basketball-shooting.html.

12. Quoted in Gilbert Rogin, "We Are Grown Men Playing a Child's Game." *Sports Illustrated*, November 18, 1963. http://sportsillustrated.cnn.com/vault/article/magazine/MAG1075395/index.htm.

13. Juan Carlos Santana. "Plyometrics Training—Part I: What It Is and What It's Not." *Perform Better*, 2009. www.performbetter.com/catalog/matriarch/OnePiecePage.asp_Q_PageID_E_58_A_PageName_E_ArticlePlyometrics1.

14. Raphael Brandon. "Prehabilitation Training Exercises," *Sports Injury Bulletin*, 2009. www.sportsinjurybulletin.com/archive/prehabilitation-exercises.html.

15. Alan Stein. "Guidelines for Year Round Injury Prevention," *Coach Like A Pro*, 2009. www.coachlikeapro.com/injury-prevention.html.

16. Quoted in NBA.com, "Williams: Team Chemistry Key to Winning," September 12, 2007. www.nba.com/knicks/news/williams_070912_interview.html.

17. Quoted in Inside Hoops.com, "Las Vegas Summer League," 2009. www.insidehoops.com/vegas-summer-league.shtml.

18. Committee on Energy and Commerce. "Testimony of David J. Stern, Commissioner, National Basketball Association." February 27, 2008. http://energycommerce.house.gov/images/stories/Documents/Hearings/PDF/110-ctcp-hrg.022708.Stern-testimony.pdf.

19. Quoted in Tim Povtak, "Rashard Lewis on 10-Game Suspension: 'I Did Nothing Wrong.'" *NBA Fanhouse*, September 28, 2009. http://nba.fanhouse.com/2009/09/28/rashard-lewis-on-10-game-suspension-i-did-nothing-wrong/.

20. Quoted in ESPN, "Anabolic Steroids," 2007. http://espn.go.com/special/s/drugsandsports/steroids.html.

21. Family Education.com. "Teen Steroid Use," 2009. http://life.familyeducation.com/athletic-training/drugs-and-alcohol/58291.html?page=2&detoured=1.

Chapter 3: Sports Medicine

22. Dan Bell. "Keeping Them Fine-Tuned," *NBA.com*, 2010. www.nba.com/timberwolves/news/Keeping_Them_FineTuned-300855-1193.html.

23. Quoted in "Kobe Shakes Off Pain of Dislocated Finger to Turn Away Cavs." *CBS Sports*, January 20, 2009. www.cbssports.com/nba/gamecenter/recap/NBA_20090119_CLE@LAL.

24. Quoted in GirlsCanJump.com, "Jump Training: Ten Ways to Protect Your Knees If You Play Sports." 2005. www.girlscanjump.com/plyometrics.html.

25. Quoted in Carla Williams, "Female Athletes Bear Brunt of Concussions." *ABC News*, October 2, 2007. http://abcnews.go.com/Health/Exercise/Story?id=3680112&page=1.

26. Quoted in Gary Washburn, "Inside the NBA: ACL Tear Takes Own Sweet Time." *Seattle PI.com*, March 30, 2007. www.seattlepi.com/basketball/309644_nban30.html.

27. Quoted in Jonathan Feigen, " Yao Out, But Not Too Down: Center Looks Forward to Rehab, Next Season." *The Houston Chronicle*, May 10, 2009, p. 4. www.chron.com/disp/story.mpl/sports/6417648.html.

28. Quoted in Tom Callahan, "Beyond the Traditional in Sports Medicine." *The New York Times*, May 10, 1998, p. 14WC19. www.nytimes.com/1998/05/10/nyregion/beyond-the-traditional-in-sports-medicine.html.

29. Quoted in David Williams, "Sports Medicine Goes High-Tech." *CNN.com*, October 25, 2006. www.cnn.com/2006/TECH/10/12/sports.medicine/index.html.

Chapter 4: High-Tech Equipment

30. Charles W. Bryant. "What Makes Sports Flooring Different." *How Stuff Works*, March 16, 2009. http://home.howstuffworks.com/home-improvement/flooring/what-makes-sports-flooring-different.htm.

31. Quoted in *Sports Business Daily*, "Slippery When Dry: NCAA Tried to Make On-Court Decal Rougher," April 1, 2008. www.sportsbusinessdaily.com/article/119693.

32. Quoted in Chris Reidy, "From Spalding, A Ball That Rarely Needs to Be Refilled." *The Boston Globe*, November 17, 2005. www.boston.com/business/articles/2005/11/17/from_spalding_a_ball_that_rarely_needs_to_be_refilled/.

33. Quoted in J. Michael Falgoust, "Neuromuscular Mouth Guard Draws Performance Debate." *USA Today*, November 17, 2009. www.usatoday.com/sports/2009-11-16-neuromuscular-mouthguard-cover_N.htm.

34. Bill Willis. "The Physics of Basketball." *Worlsey School Online*, 2009. www.worsleyschool.net/science/files/physicsof/basketball.html.

Chapter 5: The Physics Behind the Moves

35. Saul Shandly. "The Physics of Basketball." *Associated Content*, July 17, 2008. www.associatedcontent.com/article/866313/the_physics_of_basketball.html?cat=14.

36. David E. Watson. "The Conservation of Energy and the First Law of Thermodynamics." *FT Exploring Science and Technology*, 2005. www.ftexploring.com/energy/first-law.html.

37. Quoted in Mick Kulikowski, "Nothing But Net: The Physics of Basketball Free Throws." *North Carolina State University*, November 3, 2009. http://news.ncsu.edu/uncategorized/161mkfreethrow/.

38. John J. Fontanella. *The Physics of Basketball*. Baltimore, MD: Johns Hopkins University Press, 2006, p. 80.

39. Fontanella, *The Physics of Basketball*, p. 72.

40. Kulikowski, "Nothing But Net."

41. Daniella Gardino. "7 Steps to Becoming a Better Foul Shooter." *Ezine Articles.com*, October 23, 2009. http://ezinearticles.com/?7-Steps-to-Becoming-a-Better-Foul-Shooter&id=3142154.

42. Quoted in Ira Berkow, ed., *Court Vision: Unexpected Views on the Lure of Basketball.* New York: Harper Collins, 2000, p. 72.
43. Willis, "The Physics of Basketball."
44. Willis, "The Physics of Basketball."
45. Joe Waters. "Basketball Rebounding—8 Qualities for Success." *Ezine Articles.com*, August 28, 2006. http://ezinearticles.com/?Basketball-Rebounding---8-Qualities-For-Success&id=284074.

Chapter 6: Bodies in Motion

46. Quoted in Ira Berkow, ed., *Court Vision*, p. 4.
47. Mark Welling. "Why I Love John Stockton's Game." *Ezine Articles.com*, September 14, 2009. http://ezinearticles.com/?Why-I-Love-John-Stocktons-Game&id=2922349.
48. Randy Brown. "Behind-The-Scenes Look at NBA's Steve Nash." *Helium*, 2009. www.helium.com/items/271819-behind-the-scenes-look-at-the-nbas-steve-nash?page=2.
49. John M. Epley. "The Balance System 101: How it Functions." *Ear Info Site*, 2007. www.midmoors.co.uk/balance/Balance101.htm.
50. Jon Oliver. *Basketball Fundamentals; A Better Way to Learn the Basics.* Champaign, IL: Human Kinetics Publishers, 2004, p. 2.
51. Denise K. Wood. "Sports Training Tips to Improve Reaction Time and Decision Making." *Articles Base.com*, September 8, 2009. www.articlesbase.com/sports-and-fitness-articles/sports-training-tips-to-improve-reaction-time-and-decision-making-1209447.html.
52. Quoted in Frank Vizard, ed., *Why a Curveball Curves: The Incredible Science of Sports.* New York: Hearst Books, 2008, p. 83.
53. Alan Goldberg. "Basketball." *Competitive Advantage*, 2009. www.competitivedge.com/sports_article_basketball.htm.

Chapter 7: The Psychology of Winning

54. Hal Wissel. "Basketball Shooting Confidence and Rhythm." *Hoops U.com*, 2009. www.hoopsu.com/coachingtips/wissel-shooting-confidence.html.
55. Quoted in Doug Ward, "Sports: Athletes with Doubts About Performance Retrained to Think Positively." Vancouver Sun, September 25, 2009. www.vancouversun.com/story_print.html?id=2035705&sponsor=.
56. Quoted in Pat Williams and Michael Weinreb, How to Be Like Mike. Deerfield Beach, FL: Health Communications, Inc., 2001, p. 105.
57. Jim Taylor. "The Power of Prime." *Psychology Today*, September 30, 2009. www.psychologytoday.com/blog/the-power-prime/200909/sports-prime-sport-pyramid.

58. Quoted in Carl Bialik, "The Power of Lucky Charms—New Research Suggests How They Really Make Us Perform Better." *The Wall Street Journal*, April 29, 2010, p. D1. http://online.wsj.com/article/SB10001424052748703648304575212361800043460.html.

59. Quoted in Bialik, "The Power of Lucky Charms," p. D1.

60. Quoted in Terry Pluto, Tall Tales: *The Glory Years of the NBA, in the Words of the Men Who Played, Coached and Built Pro Basketball.* New York: Simon and Schuster, 1992, p. 277.

61. Quoted in Brad Winters, "Basketball Coaching Quotes: Basketball Inspirational and Motivational Quotes." *Coach Like A Pro.com*, 2009. www.coachlikeapro.com/basketball-coaching-quotes.html.

62. Quoted in *Sports Illustrated*, "A Dark Side of Knight: Ex-Hoosiers Speak in *CNN/Sports Illustrated* Exclusive." CNN/Sports Illustrated, September 10, 2000. http://sportsillustrated.cnn.com/thenetwork/news/2000/03/14/knight_indiana/.

63. Quoted in Chris Broussard, "X Marks the Spot of Greatest NBA Coach." *ESPN.com*, June 15, 2009. http://sports.espn.go.com/nba/playoffs/2009/columns/story?columnist=broussard_chris&page=philjax-090615.

64. Quoted in Berkow, *Court Vision*, p. 169.

65. Quoted in Alexander Wolff, *100 Years of Hoops.* Birmingham, AL: Oxmoor House, 1993, p. 110.

66. Quoted in Williams and Weinreb, *How to Be Like Mike*, p. 211.

67. James Naismith. "Basketball Quotes." *Quote Mountain.com*, 2005. www.quotemountain.com/quotes/sports_quotes/basketball_quotes.

GLOSSARY

acceleration: The change in velocity of an object over time.

arc: A segment of a circle, shaped like a curve.

concussion: Injury to the brain caused by a blow, a fall, or violent shaking.

energy: The ability of a physical system to do work.

friction: The force that resists motion when the surface of one object comes into contact with the surface of another.

inertia: The tendency of an object to stay at rest or stay moving as long as it is not acted on by an outside force.

hang time: The moment that basketball players seem to float in the air when they jump.

ligament: Fibrous tissue that connects one bone to another bone.

mass: The quantity of matter in an object.

prehabilitation: Training before playing a sport that reduces the risk of injuries.

projectile: An object that once started by a force continues in motion by its own inertia and is influenced only by the downward force of gravity.

stress fracture: A crack in a bone caused by repeated stress.

tendon: Fibrous tissue that connects a muscle to a bone.

velocity: Measure of the speed and direction of a body in motion.

FOR MORE INFORMATION

Books

John Eric Goff. *Gold Medal Physics: The Science of Sports*. Baltimore, MD: The Johns Hopkins University Press, 2010. A discussion of some basic physics concepts in sports.

Madeline Goodstein. *Sports Science Projects: The Physics of Balls in Motion*. Berkeley Heights, NJ: Enslow Publishers, 1999. Includes experiments with balls that answer questions such as "How does one control the bounciness of a basketball?"

Salvatore Tocci. *Experiments with Sports*. New York: Children's Press, 2003. The book includes a variety of simple science experiments that demonstrate scientific principles behind sports moves.

Bobby Mercer. *The Leaping, Sliding, Sprinting, Riding Science Book: 50 Super Sports Science Activities*. Asheville, NC: Lark Books, 2007. An unusual physics book in which the author includes a list of equipment and instructions for performing activities, followed by a section that explains the science behind it.

Websites

All American Red Heads, 1936–1986 (www.allamericanredheads.com). Information, photos, and a video about one of the most colorful women's basketball teams in America.

Black Fives (www.blackfives.com). A complete source for photos, videos, and the history of black fives teams.

Hoopedia (http://hoopedia.nba.com/index.php?title=Main_Page). An online encyclopedia of basketball that covers the NBA, college leagues, basketball movies, stamps, and everything else of interest to fans.

The Physics of Basketball (http://mrfizzix.com/basketball). A website that covers physics concepts involved in the sport of basketball.

INDEX

PICTURE CREDITS

ABOUT THE AUTHOR

Diane Yancey lives in the Pacific Northwest with her husband, Michael, and their cats, Newton, Lily, and Alice. She has written more than twenty-five books for middle-grade and high school readers, including *The Forensic Anthropologist*, *The Forensic Entomologist*, *The Case of the Green River Killer*, *The Unabomber*, and *The Zodiac Killer*.